The Random House Guide to Grammar, Usage, and Punctuation

The
Random
Guide

House

to GRAMMAR, USAGE, and PUNCTUATION

Laurie Rozakis, Ph.D.

 **RANDOM HOUSE**

Random House publications are available at special discounts for corporate use, in bulk purchases of one hundred copies or more for promotions or premiums. Special editions, including personalized covers and corporate imprints, can be created in large quantities for special needs. For more information, write to the Director of Special Markets, Random House, Inc., 201 East 50th Street, New York, NY 10022.

Library of Congress Cataloging-in-Publication Data
Rozakis, Laurie.
The Random House guide to grammar, usage, and punctuation/Laurie Rozakis.
p. cm. 0-394-58920-3
ISBN
1. English language—Grammar—1950- 2. English language—Punctuation. 3. English language—Usage.
I. Title.
PE112.R69 1990
428.2—dc20   90-33069

Manufactured in the United States of America
9 8 7 6 5
First Edition
New York Toronto London Sydney Auckland

Contents

Section I

Grammar

Parts of Speech

Your ability to communicate ideas clearly and effectively depends on your understanding of and familiarity with English grammar. Grammatical rules and terms help define the construction of our language and show us how to use words correctly in written and spoken English.

The English language is made up of eight basic types of words, or parts of speech: nouns, pronouns, verbs, adjectives, adverbs, prepositions, conjunctions, and interjections. Our review will explain how parts of speech are arranged in structures that form the basis of speech and writing.

The part of speech is determined by the way a word is used in a sentence.

Words often serve more than one grammatical function, depending on their placement within sentences. Therefore, the same word can be a different part of speech in different sentences. For example, the word "help" can function as both a noun and a verb, according to its use in a sentence.

"Help" *as a noun:*

The offer of *help* was greatly appreciated.
(Here "help" is a thing.)

"Help" *as a verb:*

They *help* the community by volunteering their time to tutor illiterate adults.
(Here "help" is an action.)

Since words can work in different ways, you must first determine how the word is functioning within a sentence before you can label it as a specific part of speech. You cannot assume that any word will always be the same part of speech and fulfill the same grammatical function.

Nouns

A noun is a word used to name a person, place, thing, or quality.

EXAMPLES:

Person	*Place*
Mary	library
Edward	yard
teacher	Ontario
American	coastline

cousin	Paris
Mr. Jones	city

Thing	*Quality*
snake	decency
flowers	bravery
justice	courage
mutiny	integrity
computer	sincerity
ballot	happiness

Some of the nouns listed above can be further classified into specific types: **Common nouns** name any of a class of people, places, or things. **Proper nouns** name specific people, places, and things.

EXAMPLES:

Common nouns	*Proper nouns*
girl	Lisa
river	Ohio River
road	Main Street

Collective nouns name groups of people or things.

EXAMPLES:

team	flock	pack
clan	tribe	committee

Mass nouns name qualities or things that cannot be counted.

EXAMPLES:

fury	strength	valor
gold	sand	flour

Compound nouns are made up of two or more words. The words may be separate, hyphenated, or combined.

EXAMPLES:

boarding pass	mother-in-law
housework	airport
runaway	schoolroom

Articles or noun markers

The words *a, an,* and *the,* which often precede nouns, are called **articles** or **noun markers**.

EXAMPLES:

an apple   **a** river   **the** child

Pronouns

A pronoun is a word used in place of a noun or a group of words functioning as a noun.

EXAMPLE:

Ellen has been working on a project for a long time. **She** spends eight hours a day on **it. Her** time is well spent, however, as **she herself** recognizes.

Antecedents

The meaning of a pronoun comes from the noun it represents. This noun is called the **antecedent.** In the above example, the antecedent of the pronoun *she* is *Ellen;* the antecedent of the pronoun *it* is *project.* As you can see, the antecedent usually comes before the pronoun in the sentence. Most pronouns have specific antecedents, but some do not.

Types of pronouns

There are different types of pronouns, depending on their function within a sentence and on their form.

Personal pronouns refer to specific people. Personal pronouns that refer to the speaker are known as **first-person pronouns;** those that refer to the person spoken to are known as **second-person pronouns;** those that refer to the person, place, or thing spoken about are known as **third-person pronouns.**

first-person (singular)
I, me, my, mine

second-person
you, your, yours

third-person
he, him, his, she, her, hers, it, its

first-person (plural)
we, us, our, ours

second person
you, yours, yours

third person
they, them, their, theirs

Intensive pronouns add emphasis to a noun or pronoun; **reflexive pronouns** show that the subject of the sentence also receives the action of the verb and adds information to a sentence. Both intensive and reflexive pronouns end in *-self* or *-selves*.

INTENSIVE AND REFLEXIVE PRONOUNS

myself	yourself
himself	herself
itself	ourselves
yourselves	themselves

EXAMPLES:

Intensive:

I **myself** have never given much thought to the matter.

Marty hung the striped wallpaper **himself.**

Reflexive:

I treated **myself** to a new pair of shoes.

Michael kept telling **himself** that it was not his fault.

Interrogative pronouns are used to introduce questions. These pronouns do not have to have a specific antecedent.

INTERROGATIVE PRONOUNS

which   what   who   whom   whose

EXAMPLES:

What did you call me for in the first place?

Whom have you called about this matter?

Mine was delicious. **Whose** was also?

Relative pronouns are used to tie together or relate groups of words. Relative pronouns begin subordinate clauses (see page 106).

RELATIVE PRONOUNS

which that who whom whose

EXAMPLES:

Debbie enrolled in the class **that** her employer recommended.

Charles has a friend **who** lives in Toronto, Canada.

Demonstrative pronouns identify specific nouns. They can be placed before or after their antecedents.

DEMONSTRATIVE PRONOUNS

this that these those

EXAMPLES:

This is the book I told you about last week.

That is a perfect place to sit down and have lunch.

Is **that** the house with the Japanese garden in the back yard?

Indefinite pronouns take the place of a noun but they do not have to have a specific antecedent.

COMMON INDEFINITE PRONOUNS

much	little
several	one
each	all
many	any
most	more
neither	nobody
no one	nothing
something	other
both	some
everybody	none
anyone	others
either	another
anything	few
anybody	everything
somebody	someone
everybody	

EXAMPLES:

Specific antecedent:

The **casserole** was so delicious that **none** was left by the end of the meal.

A **few** of the **relatives** usually lend a hand when my husband undertakes one of his home repair projects.

No specific antecedent:

Someone arrived at the party early, much

to the embarrassment of the unprepared host and hostess.

Everyone stayed late, too.

Case

The majority of English words rely on their position within a sentence rather than their form to show their function. In most instances, the placement of a word determines whether it is a subject or object. Certain nouns and pronouns, however, change their form to indicate their use.

Case is the form a noun or pronoun assumes that shows how it is used in a sentence.

English has three cases: **nominative, objective,** and **possessive.** In general, pronouns take the nominative case when they function as the subject of a sentence or clause and the objective case when they function as the object of a verb or preposition. Pronouns and nouns take the possessive case to indicate ownership.

Nouns change form only in the possessive case: for example, *a dog's bark, Maria's hair.* Some pronouns, in contrast, change form in the nominative, objective, and possessive cases. The following chart shows how personal pronouns change form in the three different cases.

PERSONAL PRONOUNS

Subject (Nominative case)	Object (Objective case)	Possessive (Possessive case)
I	me	my, mine
you	you	you
he	him	his
she	her	her, hers
it	it	its
we	us	our, ours
they	them	their, theirs
who	whom	whose
whoever	whomever	whoever

NOMINATIVE CASE

The nominative case is sometimes called the "subjective" case because it is used when pronouns function as subjects. The following examples illustrate how personal pronouns are used in the nominative case.

EXAMPLES OF PERSONAL PRONOUNS IN THE NOMINATIVE CASE:

Subject of a verb:

We understand that **they** will be late.

Neither **she** nor **I** will be attending.

Who is responsible for this situation?

Subject of a clause:

Give a tip to the waitress **who** helped us.

Whoever wants extra hours must see me today.

She is the person **who** recommended the plan.

Appositive identifying a subject (An appositive is a word or a phrase appearing next to a noun or pronoun that explains or identifies it and is equivalent to it:

Both physicists, Marie Curie and **he,** worked on isolating radium.

Both community members, Ellen Kessleman and **she,** traveled to Albany this weekend to lobby for increased state aid.

Predicate nominative:

It is **I.**

The primary supervisor is **she.**

The fastest runners are Lenore and **he.**

We Malones are fond of traveling.

The **predicate nominative** is the noun or pronoun after a linking verb that renames the subject. As a general rule, the linking verb *to* *be* functions as an equals sign: the words on either side must be in the same form.

Since the predicate nominative can sound overly formal in speech, many people use the colloquial: It's *me*. It's *her*. It must be *them*. In formal speech and edited writing, however, the nominative forms are used: It must be *they*. The figure at the door had been *she*, not her husband. In some instances, revising the sentence can produce a less artificial sound:

EXAMPLES:

Predicate nominatives:

The delegates who represented the community at last evening's town board meeting were **you** and **I**.

Revision:

You and **I** represented the community at last evening's town board meeting.

OBJECTIVE CASE

The objective case is used when a personal pronoun is a direct object, indirect object, or object of a preposition.

EXAMPLES:

Direct object:

Bob's jokes embarrassed **me**.

When you reach the station, call either **him** or **me**.

Indirect object:

The glaring sun gave my friends and **us** a headache.

My aunt sent **me** a scarf from Venice.

Please give **him** some money.

Object of a preposition:

From **whom** did you receive this card?

They fully understood why they had come with **us** rather than with **him**.

Let's keep this understanding between you and **me**.

Note: The nominative case is not always used after "to be." Since words on either side of *to be* are always in the same form, when the subject of an infinitive is in the objective case, the word following the infinitive is also in the objective case.

EXAMPLE:

We believed the author of the report to be **her**.

With **than** *or* **as**

If the word following *than* or *as* begins a clause, the pronoun takes the nominative case. If the word following *than* or *as* does not introduce a clause, the pronoun takes the objective case. In some instances, the case depends on the meaning of the sentence. To help decide whether the sentence requires a pronoun in the nominative or objective case, complete the clause.

EXAMPLES:

She has been working at Smithson longer than **he** (has).

Kevin is more proficient at marketing than **I** (am).

They are going to be informed as quickly as **we** (were).

I have stayed with Julia as long as **she** (has stayed with her).

I have stayed with Julia as long as **her** [as I have stayed with her].

USES OF *WHO* AND *WHOM*

The form of the pronoun **who** depends on its function within a clause, not within the sentence as a whole.

Subordinate clauses and **who/whom**

In subordinate clauses, use *who/who-ever* for all subjects, *whom/whomever* for all objects.

In subordinate clauses, use *who* and *whoever* for all subjects, *whom* and *whomever* for all objects, regardless of whether the clause itself acts as a subject or object.

EXAMPLES:

Distribute the food to **whoever** needs it.
(Since *whoever* is the subject of "needs," it is in the nominative case. Note that the entire clause *whoever needs it* is the subject of the preposition *to*.)

We did not realize **whom** the specialist called.
(Since *whom* is the object of "called," it is in the objective case. Note that the entire clause *whom the specialist called* is the object of the verb "realize.")

Frederick is the lawyer **whom** most people hire for this type of work.
(Since *whom* is the object of "hire," it is in the objective case. The clause *whom most people hire for this type of work* describes the noun "lawyer.")

Questions and **who/whom**

Use *who* at the beginning of a question about a subject; use *whom* at the beginning of a question about an object.

In speech, this distinction is often not made, and *who* is used for the first word of a question, regardless of whether the question is about a subject or an object.

To determine whether to use *who* or *whom*, use a personal pronoun to construct an answer to the question. The case of the personal pronoun determines whether *who* (nominative) or *whom* (objective) is required.

EXAMPLES:

Who left the car doors open?
(Sample answer to the question: "*He* left the car doors open." Since *he* is in the nominative case, the question is about a subject and thus requires *who*.)

Whom should I see about this invoice?
(Sample answer to the question: "You should see *him*." Since *him* is in the objective case, the question is about an object and thus requires *whom*.)

POSSESSIVE CASE

A pronoun takes the possessive case when it shows ownership.

With nouns

Use the possessive case before nouns to show ownership.

EXAMPLES:

Joan left **her** coat in the movie theater.

Theirs is the store on the corner.

Our puppy cut **its** front paw on a rough brick.

Is that book really **his**?

With gerunds

Use the possessive case before gerunds in most instances.

A gerund is the *-ing* form of the verb (examples: *swimming, snoring*) used as a noun. Possessive pronouns and nouns often precede gerunds, as in *The landlord objected to my* (not *me*) *having guests late at night.* In practice, however, both objective and possessive forms appear before gerunds.

EXAMPLES:

My shoveling the snow no doubt saved the postal carrier a nasty fall.

Do you mind **my** eating the rest of the cake?

She wholeheartedly supported **his** exercising.

My colleagues were really annoyed by **my** coughing.

A possessive is not used before a gerund when it would create a clumsy sentence. In these instances, rewrite the sentence to eliminate the awkward construction.

EXAMPLES:

The neighbors on the corner spread the news about **somebody's** wanting to organize a block party.

We heard the news that **somebody** wants to organize a block party.

In a noun position

Some possessive pronouns—*mine, his, hers, your, ours, theirs*—can be used alone in a noun position to indicate possession.

EXAMPLES:

This idea was **mine,** not yours.

Is this article really **hers?**

Do you believe that it's **theirs?**

Note: Never use an apostrophe with a possessive personal pronoun. The following personal

pronouns are already possessive so have no
need for an apostrophe: *my, mine, your, yours,
her, hers, its, our, ours, their,* and *theirs.* In
addition, do not confuse the contraction *it's*
with the possessive pronoun *its.*

AMBIGUOUS REFERENCES

Make sure that the reference is clear when
two pronouns could logically refer to either of
two antecedents. The following examples
demonstrate how ambiguities can occur.

UNCLEAR:

The manager told Mrs. Greenberger that she
will have to train her new people by June.

As the sentence is written, it is unclear
whether the manager or Mrs. Greenberger
will have to train the new people, and whose
new people have to be trained.

CLEARER:

Since Mrs. Greenberger will have to train
her new people by June, she decided to
take her vacation early in the year.

If the reference to an antecedent is not specific, confusion can arise. An unclear pronoun

reference can be usually be clarified by rearranging the sentence or by using the noun rather than the pronoun, as the following examples show.

UNCLEAR:

When you have finished with the stamp and bound the report, please return it to the storeroom.

CLEARER:

When you have finished with the stamp and bound the report, please return the stamp to the storeroom.

Sometimes, using *it, they,* or *you* incorrectly will result in a sentence that is vague or wordy. Removing the pronoun, eliminating excess words, or revising the sentence usually produces a clearer and more vigorous style.

WORDY:

In the cookbook it says that wooden chopping boards should be disinfected with bleach.

BETTER:

The cookbook says that wooden chopping boards should be disinfected with bleach.

WORDY:

They say you should use a cold steam vaporizer instead of the traditional hot steam one.

BETTER:

The doctor says we should use a cold steam vaporizer instead of the traditional hot steam one.

Verbs

A verb is a word that expresses an action, an occurrence, or a state of being.

EXAMPLES:

Action	Occurrence	State of being
jump	become	be
swim	happen	seem
jog	drop	am
think	decide	was

Action verbs can describe mental as well as physical actions. The verb *think* from the above chart, for example, describes a mental action, one that cannot be seen. Additional examples of action verbs that describe unseen mental actions include *understand, welcome, enjoy, relish, ponder, consider,* and *deliberate.*

Action verbs are divided into two groups, depending on how they function within a sentence. The division is based on whether they can stand alone or require a direct object.

Transitive verbs require a direct object. **Intransitive** verbs do not require a direct object.

EXAMPLES:

Transitive:

My son **ate** the slice of chocolate cake I was saving for my midnight snack.

My sister **promised** to bake me another cake as soon as she had a chance.

I **decided** to hold her to her promise, because she makes the best chocolate cake around.

Intransitive:

My unsympathetic husband **shrugged.**

When they heard about it, my friends **laughed.**

Worst of all, even the baby **giggled**.

Many verbs can be either transitive or intransitive, depending on their function within the sentence. To check whether a verb requires an object, try to complete the sentence by asking "what?" or "whom?" The verb is transitive if your question was answered by the sentence. Consult a dictionary to check specific words.

EXAMPLES:

Transitive:

José **eats** dinner every night at 5:45.

Intransitive:

José **eats** at regular times.

Verbs that describe an occurrence or a state of being are called **linking verbs**.

Linking verbs connect parts of a sentence.

The most common linking verbs are forms of the verb *to be*. A number of other linking verbs are also commonly used.

EXAMPLES:

To be:

am	are	is
was	were	am being
are being	is being	was being
can be	could be	may be
might be	must be	shall be
have been	might have been	may have been

Other verbs:

look	grow	sound
appear	taste	smell
become	happen	remain
stay	seem	feel

EXAMPLES:

The milk **smelled** sour.

The supports **looked** fragile.

The actor **seemed** nervous when the play began.

The verb *to be,* in common with the other words on the list, does not always function as a linking verb. To determine whether the word is functioning as a linking verb or as an action verb, examine its role within the sentence.

EXAMPLE:

Linking verb:

The child **grew** tired by the end of the evening.

Action verb:

The child **grew** three inches last year.

The **predicate nominative** is the noun or pronoun after a linking verb that renames the subject. As a general rule, the linking verb (*to be*) functions as an equals sign: the words on both sides must be in the same form.

EXAMPLES:

We all assumed that **it** was **he.**

I am waiting for mother to call. Is **that she?**

There is a third kind of verb whose function is to connect individual verbs into verb phrases.

Helping verbs combine verbs to form verb phrases.

In addition to forms of *to be*, a number of other words can function as helping verbs. These include *do, does, did, has, had, have, would, will, shall, should, must, might, may, could, can.* Helping verbs are also known as **auxiliary verbs**

EXAMPLES:

Helping verbs:

Did you complete the project on time?

May **has** seen the program before.

Have you ever eaten in that restaurant.

Helping verbs forming verb phrases:

They **might have considered** my feelings in the matter.

When **will** they **be completing** their chores?

The machine operator **should** not **have been working** when he was so fatigued.

Verb forms, tense, mood, and voice

FORMS

All English verbs except *to be* have four basic forms: the **infinitive,** the **past,** the **past participle,** and the **present participle.** Each is explained in the chart below.

Basic Verb Forms

Verb form

Infinitive

Definition	Examples
The basic form found in the dictionary	(to) grin
	(to) talk
	(to) snore
	(to) walk
	(to) drop

Verb form

Past tense

Definition	Examples
Indicates that the verb's action occurred in the past Regular verbs add *-d* or *-ed* to the infinitive	grinned
	talked
	snored
	walked
	dropped

Verb form

Past participle

Definition	Examples
Used with *have, had, has* Used with form of *to be* in the passive voice Regular forms same as past tense	grinned
	talked
	snored
	walked
	dropped

Verb form

Present participle

Definition	*Examples*
Add *-ing* to infinitive	grinning
Can combine with form of *to*	talking
be to show continuing action	snoring
	walking
	dropping

IRREGULAR VERBS

The majority of English verbs are regular and change their form by adding *-ing, -ed,* or *-d* to the infinitive. However, a substantial number of verbs do not follow this pattern. These **irregular verbs** form in their past tense and past participle in a number of different ways: some change an internal vowel and add *-n* to the past participle; some retain the same form in all three forms or in the past tense and past participle; some follow no discernible pattern.

The following list includes the most common irregular verbs. For information about verbs not included below, consult a dictionary. If a verb is regular, the dictionary will list only the infinitive. If the verb is irregular, the dictionary will include the past tense and past participle along with the infinitive; if only two forms are listed, then the past tense and the past participle are identical.

Present tense	Past tense	Past participle
arise	arose	arisen
be	was/were	been
bear	bore	borne, born
beat	beat	beaten
become	became	become
begin	began	begun
bend	bent	bent
bet	bet, betted	bet
bid	bid, bade	bid, bidden
bind	bound	bound
bite	bit	bitten
blow	blew	blown
break	broke	broken
bring	brought	brought
burn	burned, burnt	burned, burnt
burst	burst	burst
buy	bought	bought
catch	caught	caught
choose	chose	chosen
cling	clung	clung
come	came	come
creep	crept	crept
cut	cut	cut
deal	dealt	dealt
dig	dug	dug
dive	dived, dove	dived

do	did	done
draw	drew	drawn
dream	dreamed, dreamt	dreamed, dreamt
drink	drank	drunk
drive	drove	driven
eat	ate	eaten
fall	fell	fallen
fight	fought	fought
find	found	found
flee	fled	fled
fling	flung	flung
fly	flew	flown
forbid	forbade, forbad	forbidden, forbid
forget	forgot	forgotten, forgot
forgive	forgave	forgiven
freeze	froze	frozen
get	got	got, gotten
give	gave	given
go	went	gone
grow	grew	grown
hang (suspend)	hung	hung
hang (execute someone)	hanged	hanged
hear	heard	heard
hide	hid	hidden
hold	held	held
keep	kept	kept

kneel	knelt	knelt
know	knew	known
lay (put down)	laid	laid
lead	led	led
lie (rest; recline)	lay	lain
lose	lost	lost
mistake	mistook	mistaken
pay	paid	paid
ride	rode	ridden
ring	rang	rung
rise	rose	risen
run	ran	run
see	saw	seen
set	set	set
sew	sewed	sewed, sewn
shake	shook	shaken
shrink	shrank	shrunk
sing	sang, sung	sung
sit	sat	sat
slay	slew	slain
speak	spoke	spoken
spend	spent	spent
spring	sprang	sprung
stand	stood	stood
steal	stole	stolen
strike	struck	struck
swear	swore	sworn
sweep	swept	swept
swim	swam	swum
take	took	taken

teach	taught	taught
tear	tore	torn
throw	threw	thrown
wake	woke, waked	woken, waked
wear	wore	worn
weep	wept	wept
win	won	won
wind	wound	wound
wring	wrung	wrung
write	wrote	written

TENSE

Tense is the verb form that indicates time of action or state of being.

Tense is different from time. The present tense, for instance, shows present time, but it can also indicate future time or a generally accepted belief.

English has three main groups of tenses: the **simple tenses** (present, past, and future), the **perfect tenses** (present perfect, past perfect, future perfect), and the **progressive tenses** (present progressive, past progressive, future progressive, present perfect progressive, past perfect progressive, and future perfect progressive).

TENSES OF REGULAR VERBS

Simple tense (present)
smile

Perfect tense
have smiled

Progressive tense
am smiling

Simple tense (past)
smiled

Perfect tense
had smiled

Progressive tense
was smiling

Simple tense (future)
will smile

Perfect tense
will smiled

Progressive tense
will be smiling

have been smiling

had been smiling

will have been smiling

The simple tenses

The simple tenses generally show that an action or state of being is taking place now, in the future, or in the past relative to the speaker or writer. The simple tenses indicate a finished, momentary, or habitual action or condition.

The present tense (I/we/you/they walk, he-she walks)

Except when the subjects are singular nouns or third-person singular pronouns, the present tense uses the infinitive form of the verb (I *walk*, you *skip*, we *jump*, they *catch*). With singular nouns or third-person singular pronouns, -*s* or -*es* is added to the infinitive (Robert *walks*, she *skips*, he *jumps*, it *catches*).

The present tense is generally used to express a number of different actions.

EXAMPLES:

To state present action:

Nick **prepares** the walls for painting.

To show present condition:

The secretary **is** efficient.

To show that an action occurs regularly:

Louise **prepares** a report every week for her supervisor.

To show a condition that occurs regularly:

The traffic **is** usually backed up on the turnpike in the evenings.

To indicate future time:

The income tax refund **arrives** tomorrow.

To state a generally held belief:

Haste **makes** waste.

To state a scientific truth:

A body in motion **tends** to stay in motion.

To discuss literary works, films, and so on:

In *Hamlet*, Claudius **poisons** his brother, **marries** his former sister-in-law, and **seizes** the throne.

The past tense (I/he/she/we/you/they walked)

With regular verbs, the past tense is formed by adding *-d* or *-ed* to the infinitive; with irregular verbs, the entire form of the verb changes. Consult the chart on page 31 for forms of irregular past-tense verbs.

EXAMPLES:

To show completed actions:

Jimmy **walked** the dog last night.

To show completed conditions:

Joan **was** very happy.

To show recurring past actions that do not extend to the present:

During World War II, Eric **saw** the fighting through the lens of a camera.

The future tense (I/he/she/we/you/they will walk)

The future is formed by using the helping verb *will* or *shall* with the infinitive form of the verb.

EXAMPLES:

To show a future action:

Tomorrow the sun **will set** at 6:45 P.M.

To show a future condition:

They **will be excited** when they see the presents.

To indicate intention:

The Board of Education has announced that

it **will begin** repairs on the town pool as soon as possible.

To show probability:

The decrease in land values in the Northeast **will** most likely **intensify.**

The perfect tenses

The perfect tenses indicate that one action was or will be finished before another action. The perfect tenses are created by using a form of the helping verb **have** with the past participle.

The present perfect (I/we/you/they have walked, he-she has walked)

There are three main uses of the present perfect.

EXAMPLES:

To show completed action:

Martin **has finished** talking to his clients.

To show past action or condition continuing now:

We **have been waiting** for a week.

To show action that occurred at an unspecified past time:

I **have reviewed** all the new procedures.

The past perfect (I/he/she/we/you/they had walked)

As with the present perfect, the past perfect has three main uses.

EXAMPLES:

To show one action or condition completed before another:

By the time her employer returned, Linda **had completed** all her assigned tasks.

To show an action that occurred before a specific past time:

By 1930, insulin **had been isolated, refined,** and **distributed.**

To show an unfilled wish:

We **had hoped** to have the camper ready by summer vacation.

The future perfect (I/he/she/we/you/they will have walked)

The future perfect has two primary uses.

EXAMPLES:

To show a future action or condition completed before another:

By the time you read this letter, Bill **will have left** Riverside for California.

To show that an action will be over by a specific future time:

By tomorrow, the bonds **will have lost** over fifty percent of their face value.

The progressive tenses

The progressive tenses show continuing action. They are created by using a form of the verb *to be* with the *-ing* form of the verb. To form questions, make negative statements, or show emphasis, a form of the helping verb *do* is used.

EXAMPLES:

Questions:

Do they **call** every Saturday?

Negative statements:

They **do** not **call** every Saturday.

Emphasis:

They **do call** every Saturday.

The present progressive (I am walking, he/she is walking, we/you/they are walking)

There are two main uses of the present progressive.

EXAMPLES:

To show continuing action or condition:

I **am finishing** the painting while my children **are suffering** from the chicken pox.

To show something is happening, although it may not be taking place at the present:

Medicine **is becoming** increasingly specialized.

The past progressive (I was walking, he/she was walking, we/you/they were walking)

As with the present progressive, the past progressive has two main uses.

EXAMPLES:

To show an action or condition continuing in the past:

She **was becoming** increasingly disenchanted with the radical diet.

To show two past actions occurring simultaneously:

Mike fell off his bicycle while he **was watching** a cat climb a tree.

The future progressive (I/he/she/we/you/they will be walking)

There are two primary uses of the future progressive.

EXAMPLES:

To show continuing future action:

The grocery store clerk **will be counting** the number of manufacturers' coupons redeemed.

To show continuing action at a specific future time:

Carol **will be traveling** to New Orleans this summer.

The present perfect progressive (I/we/you/they have been walking, he/she has been walking)

The present perfect progressive is used only to show that an action or condition is continuing from the past into the present and/or the future.

EXAMPLE:

The amount of pollution **has been increasing** sharply.

The past perfect progressive (I/he/she/we/ you/they had been walking)

The past perfect progressive is used only to show that a continuing past action has been interrupted by another.

EXAMPLE:

Stephan **had been visiting** the museum that was torn down to make way for condominiums.

The future perfect progressive (I/he/she/we/ you/they will have been walking)

The future perfect progressive is used only to show that an action or condition will continue until a specific time in the future.

EXAMPLE:

By Monday, I **will have been working** on that project for a month.

Using tenses

Use the appropriate sequence of verb tenses.

This refers to the relationship among the verbs within a sentence. For clarity and sense, all the verbs within a sentence must accurately reflect changes in time.

Simultaneous actions

Sometimes all the action described by each verb in a sentence occurs at approximately the same time. In such instances, the tenses of all the verbs within a sentence will usually be the same.

EXAMPLE:

When one-year-old Jessica **blew** out the candles, her parents **rose, clapped,** and **cheered.**

Actions occurring at different times

Many times, however, the verbs within a sentence describe actions that have occurred, are occurring, or will occur at different times. In these instances, the tenses of the verbs will be different to express the different time sequence.

In general, the tenses of verbs in independent adjacent clauses can shift as necessary to convey meaning and maintain logic.

The hearing **was** not well controlled, but the election **will show** whether the community will continue to oppose the rezoning plans.

In many instances, however, the tenses of verbs in subordinate clauses or verbal phrases depend on the tense of the verb in the independent clause. The following guidelines are generally followed to ensure logical sentences.

If the verb in the main clause is in the past tense, verbs in subordinate clauses are usually in the past or past perfect.

Since the verb in the main clause refers to an action already finished, it is logical for the actions in the subordinate clauses to be completed as well, as the following examples show.

Main clause

William Carlos Williams *was* a pediatrician in Paterson, New Jersey

Subordinate clause

who *wrote* some of the most distinctive verse of the twentieth century.

Main Clause

The movie *had ended*

Subordinate clause

by the time the pizzas *were delivered*.

Main clause

The conference *was* over

Subordinate clause

by the time I *arrived*.

Use infinitives logically.

The present infinitive (*to do, to tell*), expresses action occurring at the same time as or later than that of the main verb. The perfect infinitive (*to have done, to have told*) expresses action occurring before that of the main verb. The following examples indicate some possible combinations of verbs.

Main verb (simultaneous actions)
I *drove*

Infinitive
to see a concert last night.

Main verb (present/future)
I *want*

Infinitive
to visit Albany next summer.

Main verb (present/present)
I *would like*

Infinitive
to attend the seminar.

Main verb (present/past)
Julia *would like*

Infinitive
to have seen Albany last year

Use participles logically.

The present participle expresses action occurring at the same time as that of the main verb. The past participle and the present perfect participle express action occurring before that of the main verb. The following examples indicate some possible combinations of verbs.

Participle (present)
Chewing his pencil absently,

Main verb
Dick *looked* into space.

Participle (past)
Having operated the terminal for a month,

Main verb

the assistant *knew* how to repair the mal-
function.

Avoid shifting unnecessarily from one tense to another.

Illogical shifts in verb tenses confuse readers and muddle meaning. Using tenses correctly allows you to express the desired
sequence of events clearly.

MOOD

In grammar, mood is the verb form that shows
the writer's or speaker's stance toward what
he or she is saying. Different moods reveal
different attitudes. In English, there are three
moods: the indicative, the imperative, and the
subjunctive.

The **indicative mood** is used to state a fact,
ask a question, or express an opinion. Using a
form of the verb *to do* with the indicative mood
adds emphasis.

EXAMPLES:

Fact:

Henry James **did write** *The Turn of the
Screw*

We **do hold** soccer games only on Saturdays.

Question:

Did T. S. Eliot **have** a great impact on twentieth-century literature?

Do we **hold** soccer games only on Saturdays?

Opinion:

My sister **does need** my advice.

The library **does have** an excellent reference section.

The **imperative mood** is used to give directions or express commands. Frequently, the subject (usually *you*) is understood rather than stated. *Let's* or *let us* can be used before the basic form of the verb in a command.

EXAMPLES:

Command:

Get up! **Let's go** to Mario's restaurant for dinner.

Directions:

Turn left at the convenience store.

The **subjunctive mood** was traditionally used to state wishes or desires, requirements, suggestions, or conditions that are contrary to fact. It was also used in clauses beginning with *that* and with certain idioms.

Although the subjunctive mood has largely disappeared from English, it survives, somewhat inconsistently, in sentences with conditional clauses contrary to fact and in subordinate clauses after verbs like *wish:* If the school budgets *were* passed, we would have built the new wing. I wish I *was* more systematic. It is also used with some idioms and set phrases, such as Far *be* it from me . . . If *need* be, . . . *Be* that as it may. The people *be* damned. *Come* rain or *come* shine. As it *were* . . . *Come* what may.

VOICE

Voice shows whether the subject of the verb acts or is acted upon. Only transitive verbs (those that take objects) can show voice.

Active voice

When the subject of the verb does the action, the sentence is said to be in the active voice: I *hit* the ball across the field. The subject, *I*, does the action, *hit*.

Passive voice

When the subject of the verb receives the action, the sentence is said to be in the passive voice: The ball *was hit* by me. The subject, *the ball*, receives the action, *was hit*.

To form the passive voice, add the appropriate form of *to be (is, was, will be, has been*, etc.) to the past participle of a verb: *is smashed, was dropped, are being removed, has been repeated, had been sent.*

To change a sentence from the active voice to the passive voice, make the direct or indirect object of the verb the subject of the verb, as shown in the following examples.

Active voice

Storms *damaged* homes.

Passive voice

The homes *were damaged* by storms.

Active voice

I *will make* dinner.

Passive voice

The dinner *will be made* by me.

Active voice

Rover *bit* Christopher.

Passive voice

Christopher *was bitten* by Rover.

Active voice

Conrad *wrote Lord Jim.*

Passive voice

Lord Jim was written by Conrad.

When to use the active voice

In general, use the active voice to emphasize the performer of the verb's action. Except for a small number of specific situations, which are explained below, the active voice is usually clearer and more powerful than the passive voice.

When to use the passive voice

The passive voice is more effective in certain situations.

EXAMPLES:

When you do not wish to mention the performer of the action:

A mistake **has been made.**

A check **has been returned** marked ''insufficient funds.''

When it is necessary to avoid vagueness:

Furniture **is manufactured** in Hickory, North Carolina.

Recasting this sentence in the active voice—
"They manufacture furniture in Hickory,
North Carolina"—results in the vague
"they.")

*When the performer of the action is not
known:*

Plans for fifty units of low-income housing
were unveiled at today's county meeting.

The computer **was stolen.**

*When the result of the action is more impor-
tant than the person performing the action:*

The driver **was arrested** for speeding.

The chief suspect **was freed** on bail pending
trial.

VERBALS

A verbal is a verb used as another part of speech.

Although verbals do not function within a sentence as verbs, they can be modified by adverbs and adverbial phrases. They can also
take a complement. Verbals can function as
nouns, adjectives, or adverbs, as the following
chart explains:

Verbals and their grammatical functions

Verbal	*Uses*
Participles	function as adjectives
Gerunds	function as nouns
Infinitives	function as adverbs, adjectives, or nouns

The **verbal phrase** is the verbal and all the words related to it.

Participial phrases function as adjectives. They can be placed before or after the word they describe: The child, *waving a bright red balloon,* stood out in the crowd.

Gerund phrases function as nouns. Gerunds always end in *-ing: Eating oat bran daily* supposedly helps people lower their cholesterol level.

Infinitive phrases can function as nouns, adjectives, or adverbs. Infinitive phrases begin with the word *to: To eat in that restaurant* is an unusual experience.

Adjectives

An adjective is a word used to describe (modify) a noun or pronoun.

Adjectives add color and detail to writing by providing more precise shades of meaning. Often, adjectives give a sentence the exactness that nouns alone cannot. They describe by telling "how many," "how much," "what kind," or "which one."

EXAMPLES:

How many?

The illness has affected **twelve** people in the apartment complex.

We could give you **additional** reasons why that would not be a wise decision, but we believe these will suffice.

How much?

"You have had **enough** cookies for one day," the mother admonished her child.

"With a **little** more money," he remarked, "we could really spruce this place up."

What kind?

The **gold** earrings match that sweater much better than the **silver** ones do.

The **eerie** noise seems to come from the basement.

Which one?

Those newspapers and **these** books can be recycled, but **that** plastic laundry basket cannot.

"This is the **fifth** time I've asked you to clean your room!" the father shouted at his son.

Placement of adjectives

An adjective can come before or after the noun or pronoun it describes. More than one adjective can be used to describe the same word.

EXAMPLES:

Before the noun:

The **red, white,** and **blue** eye shadow proclaimed her patriotism but did little for her appearance.

After the noun:

The caretaker, **ill** with fever, was unable to carry out his duties.

Nouns and pronouns as adjectives

Nouns and pronouns can function as adjectives as well.

EXAMPLES:

The **produce** stall is open all night.

He has always enjoyed **piano** concertos.

We look forward to our **morning** coffee break.

Common phrases in which nouns are used as adjectives

apple pie	flood control
truth serum	child care
amusement park	art history
beach towel	dance class
flower bed	horse trailer
Star Wars	water color

The **personal pronouns** *my, your, his, her, its, our, their;* the **demonstrative pronouns** *this, that, these, those;* the **interrogative pronouns** *which, what, that;* and the **indefinite adjectives** *some, another, both, few, many, most, more,* etc. can all function as adjectives as well.

EXAMPLES:

Personal pronouns:

Did she ask for **her** superior's approval?

The team tried to give **its** support to the sidelined player.

Demonstrative adjectives:

Are **those** socks yours or his?

This bus is rarely on time in the winter.

Interrogative adjectives:

Which chores do you dislike the least?

What hobbies and sports do you enjoy the most?

Indefinite adjectives:

Some people have managed to get tickets for the concert.

Anyone who wanted tickets had to be at the stadium at 4:00 A.M.

Special adjectives

There are also three special kinds of adjectives: **proper adjectives, compound adjectives,** and **articles.**

A proper noun used as an adjective or an adjective formed from a proper noun is called a **proper adjective.** Many of these adjectives are forms of people's names, as in 'Emersonian,'' from the nineteenth-century writer Ralph Waldo Emerson. Others come from places, such as ''Florida'' oranges or ''New Zealand'' kiwis.

An adjective made up of two or more words is called a **compound adjective.** The words in a compound adjective may be combined or hyphenated.

The **articles** or **noun markers** *a, an,* and *the* are also considered adjectives. *The* is called the **definite article;** *a* and *an* are called **indefinite articles.** Use *a* before consonant sounds; *an* before vowel sounds, not letters. See pages 5 and 177 for further guidelines on the usage of articles.

Proper adjectives	*Compound adjectives*
Kafkaesque realism (Kafka)	nearsighted
Shavian wit (Shaw)	soft-shelled
Italian food	open-and-shut
Chinese silks	hard-working
March wind	close-by

Articles

a brick
a union
an elephant
an honest deal
the deal

Using adjectives

In general, use an adjective after a linking verb.

A linking verb connects a subject with its complement, a descriptive word. The words that follow linking verbs are called **subject complements.** The words most frequently used as linking verbs include: forms of *to be, (is, am, are, was, were);* such as *appear, seem, believe, become, grow, turn, prove, remain;* and sensory verbs such as *sound, look, hear, smell, feel,* and *taste.*

The function of the verb within the sentence determines whether it is a linking verb or not. Use an adjective when the modifier describes the subject. When the modifier describes the verb rather than the subject, it is an adverb.

EXAMPLES:

Adjective after a linking verb:

The dog smelled **bad** after he fell into the garbage can.

The dog appeared **brave.**

Adverb:

The cats messed up the front yard **badly.**

Roger stood **bravely.**

Generally, after a direct object use an adverb to modify the verb; use an adjective to modify the object.

If the verb's direct object is followed by a word that describes the verb, the word must be an adverb: He **mumbled** the **words** quietly.

verb ... *dir. obj.* ... *describes verb*

On the other hand, if the direct object is followed by a word that describes the object, the word must be an adjective: Soft music **made** the **dog** quiet.

verb ... *dir. obj.* ... *modifies dir. obj.*

EXAMPLES:

Adjective after a direct object:

His mother **called him quiet.** (His mother thought he was quiet.)

verb dir. obj. adjective ... *modifies dir. obj.*

The evaluation committee **considered** the firm's **work complete.** (The evaluation committee believed that the firm had finished all its work.)

verb ... *dir. obj. adjective* ... *modifies dir. obj.*

Adverb after a direct object:

His mother **called him quietly.** (His mother called him in a hushed voice.)

verb dir. obj. adverb ... *modifies verb*

The evaluation committee **considered** the firm's **work completely.** (The evaluation committee evaluated the firm's work in its entirety.)

verb ... *dir. obj. adverb* ... *describes verb*

Adverbs

An adverb is a word used to describe a verb, an adjective, or another adverb.

Like adjectives, adverbs add description and detail to writing by more closely focusing the meaning of a verb, an adjective, or another adverb. They can sometimes provide a wider range of description than adjectives alone. They describe by telling "where," "when," "how," or "to what extent."

EXAMPLES:

Where?

The pot boiled **over.**

The rain came **down.**

When?

Yesterday, I banned soda from the house; **today,** I rescinded the edict.

The children **often** speak about my instant edicts.

How?

I **quickly** changed the topic.

Life **slowly** returns to normal, but the dog moves **cautiously.**

To what extent?

Wash your hands **completely,** please.

The child has **fully** recovered from the experience.

Placement of adverbs

An adverb can come before or after the verb it describes. It can also come before, after, or in a verb phrase.

EXAMPLES:

Adverb before the verb;

Today I have to get to the bank, food store, and laundry.

Adverb after the verb:

Wendy liked to run **briskly** for twenty minutes every morning.

Adverb in a verb phrase:

Judging from the relatively minor damage, the fire fighters must have responded **quickly** when the fire alarm sounded.

Words that can be either adjectives or adverbs

Depending on how they are used, some words can function as both adjectives or adverbs.

EXAMPLES:

Adverb:

I was so exhausted that I went to bed **early**.

Jeannine is fortunate that she lives **close** to public transportation.

Adjective:

I had an **early** appointment this morning.

That sure was a **close** call!

Distinguishing adverbs from adjectives

Many adverbs end in -*ly*, but this is not a reliable way to distinguish adverbs from adjectives, because there are some adjectives that end in -*ly*, as well as some adverbs that have two different forms. As illustrated above, determine the type of word by its position in the sentence, not by its ending. The following chart shows some adjectives and adverbs that end in -*ly*.

EXAMPLES:

Adjectives that end in -**ly**	*Adverbs that end in* -**ly**
curly tail	paint quickly
surly child	color brightly
lovely picture	ate poorly

Further, some adverbs have two forms, one that ends in *-ly* and one that does not.

Some common adverbs that have two forms

cheap, cheaply	high, highly	late, lately
loud, loudly	near, nearly	quick, quickly
sharp, sharply	slow, slowly	wrong, wrongly

In some instances, the choice of form depends on the idiomatic use of the word. *Nearly,* for example, is used to mean "almost," while *near* is used to mean "close in time": Summer is drawing *near* (close in time). Summer is *nearly* (almost) arrived. Today, *slow* is used chiefly in spoken commands with short verbs that express motion, such as *drive* and *run* (Drive slow) and combined with present participles to form adjectives (He was *slow-moving*). *Slowly* is commonly found in writing, and is used in both speech and writing before a verb (He *slowly* swam across the cove) as well as after (He swam *slowly* through the waves).

In general, the short forms are used more often in informal writing and speech; the long forms more often in formal discourse.

Using adjectives and adverbs to make comparisons

Many adjectives and adverbs take different forms when they are used to make comparisons. The three forms are the **positive,** the **comparative,** and the **superlative.**

POSITIVE DEGREE

The positive degree is the basic form of the adjective or the adverb, the form listed in the dictionary. Since the positive degree does not indicate any comparison, the adjective or adverb does not change form.

COMPARATIVE DEGREE

The comparative form indicates a greater degree by comparing two things. In the comparative form, adjectives and adverbs add *-er* or *more.*

SUPERLATIVE DEGREE

The superlative form indicates the greatest degree of difference or similarity by generally comparing three or more things. In this form, adjectives and adverbs add *-est* or *most.*

WHEN TO USE *LESS/LEAST/MORE/MOST* OR *-ER/-EST*

A number of one- and two-syllable adjectives and adverbs use *-er* to form the comparative degree and *-est* to form the superlative degree. In some instances, these words use *more* and *most* when necessary to avoid awkwardness.

EXAMPLES:

Positive form (1 syllable)
blue   poor   rich

Comparative form
bluer   poorer   richer

Superlative form
bluest   poorest   richest

Positive form (2 syllables)
pretty   heavy   steady

Comparative form
prettier   heavier   steadier

Superlative form
prettiest   heaviest   steadiest

Positive form (more/most)
child-like   youthful   golden

Comparative form
more child-like   more youthful   more golden

Superlative form
most child-like   most youthful   most golden

In general, most adjectives and adverbs of more than three syllables and nearly all adverbs ending in *ly* use *more/less* and *most/least* to form the comparative and superlative degrees.

EXAMPLES:

Positive (more than three syllables)
regular   customary   admiring

Comparative
more regular   less customary   more admiring

Superlative
most regular   least customary   most admiring

Positive (-ly endings)
slow   harsh   rude

Comparative
more slowly   less harshly   more rudely

Superlative
most slowly   least harshly   most rudely

Despite the above guidelines, there are a number of words that can add either -er/-est or more/most to form the comparative and superlative degrees. The word *steady* is a case in point. The comparative can be either *steadier* or *more steady:* the superlative can be either *steadfast* or *most steady.* Some writes feel *more* and *most* place more emphasis on the comparison.

For further reference, consult the dictionary. Comparatives and superlatives formed with -er and -est will be listed in the dictionary. Those that are not included are formed with *more* and *most.*

IRREGULAR ADJECTIVES AND ADVERBS

A number of adverbs and adjectives are irregular in the comparative and superlative degrees, as shown in the chart below.

Positive Adverbs	*Comparative Adverbs*	*Superlative Adverbs*
well	better	best
badly	worse	worst

Positives Adjectives	*Comparative Adjectives*	*Superlative Adjectives*
good	better	best
bad	worse	worst

| little | little, less | little, least |
| many, some, much | more | most |

COMPARATIVE VERSUS SUPERLATIVE

In general, use the comparative form to compare two or more things; use the superlative form to compare three or more things.

EXAMPLES:

Comparative:

He was the **smarter** of the two hamsters.

Marc was the **bigger** of the two second-graders.

Louis is the **quicker** of two runners.

Superlative:

Of the six hamsters, Twiddles is the **smartest**.

Among the six of you, Roberta Sue is the **biggest.**

Of all the runners, Louis is the **quickest.**

DOUBLE COMPARISONS

Avoid using double comparatives or double superlatives: *-er* cannot be combined with *more* or *less*; *-est* cannot be combined with *most* or *least*.

EXAMPLES:

Amanda gets a bigger allowance because she is **older** (not "more older") than I am.

She is the **nicest** (not "most nicest") student I have this semester.

ABSOLUTES CANNOT BE COMPARED FURTHER

There are a number of words whose positive degree describes their only form. Words such as *central, dead, empty, excellent, impossible, infinite, perfect, straight,* and *unique* cannot have a greater or lesser degree. Therefore, something cannot be "more unique" or "most infinite." Increasingly, however, this distinction is not followed in informal speech.

In general, avoid using comparative or superlative forms for adjectives and adverbs that cannot be compared.

COMPARISON OF LIKE OBJECTS

Balance sentences by comparing like objects.

Comparing dissimilar things can result in illogical and awkward sentences.

EXAMPLES:

Weak:

Cooking with herbs is more healthful than fat.

Better:

Cooking with herbs is more healthful than **cooking** with fat.

Weak:

His comic book collection is larger than his friend's.

Better:

His comic book collection is larger than his friend's **comic book collection.**

OTHER AND ELSE

One way to avoid awkward and meaningless comparisons is to include either *other* or *else* when comparing one element of a group to the rest of the group. Without these words, you are in effect comparing the item to itself.

In general, use *other* or *else* when comparing one member of a group to the other members of the group.

EXAMPLES:

Weak:

Their landscaping is nicer than any in the neighborhood.

Better:

Their landscaping is nicer than any **other** in the neighborhood.

Weak:

That little boy hits better than anyone on the Little League team.

Better:

That little boy hits better than anyone **else** on the Little League team.

Prepositions

A preposition is a word used to connect a noun or pronoun to another word in the sentence.

Prepositions can be single or compound words.

Common prepositions and prepositional phrases

about	above	according to
across	after	against
ahead of	along	along with
amid	among	apart from
around	as of	as regards
as to	aside from	at
because of	before	behind
below	beneath	beside
besides	between	beyond
but	by	by means of
by reason of	by way of	concerning
despite	down	due to
during	except for	excepting
for	from	in
in addition to	in back of	in case of
in front of	in lieu of	in place of
in regard to	inside	in spite of
instead of	into	in view of
like	near	next to
of	off	on
on account of	onto	opposite
out	out of	outside
over	owing to	past
prior to	regarding	round
since	through	throughout
till	to	toward
under	underneath	unlike
until	up	upon

up to	with	with refer- ence to
with regard to	with respect to	with the ex- ception of
within	without	

Prepositional phrases

Since a preposition functions to connect a subject to the rest of the sentence, it is often followed by either a noun or a pronoun. The group of words opening with a preposition and ending with a noun or pronoun is called a **prepositional phrase.** The **object of the preposition** is the noun or pronoun at the end of the phrase.

A prepositional phrase can be made up of any number of words, depending on the length of the sentence.

EXAMPLES:

toward the mountain

away from the ocean

by the side of the cliff

in front of the bushes

on account of his gross negligence

around the bottom

Placement of prepositions

Since a preposition connects a subject to the rest of the sentence, it should logically be followed by either a noun or a pronoun. Traditionally, grammar guides taught that it was incorrect to end a sentence with a preposition. Nevertheless, today the practice of ending sentences with prepositions is commonly accepted.

EXAMPLES:

What did Linda do that **for**?

Josh and Carol had many things to talk **about**.

A preposition normally comes before its object, but sometimes, especially in speech, the preposition comes after its object.

EXAMPLES:

Preposition before the object:

For a week, she couldn't get the horrible scene out of her mind.

In addition to his superb academic record, he was an outstanding athlete and humanitarian.

Preposition after the object:

What do you want to do that **for**?

We know which **chair** you are **behind**!

Prepositional phrases as adverbs and adjectives

Since prepositions relate words, prepositional phrases can function as adverbs or adjectives. In this role, prepositional phrases add description and color to writing. In addition, prepositional phrases can function as nouns.

EXAMPLES:

Prepositional phrase as adverb:

He hammered rapidly **underneath the overhang despite the unseasonable heat.**

The children fly their new dragon kite **in the wide open field.**

Prepositional phrase as adjective:

Melinda is the girl **with the missing front tooth.**

Living **in a big city** affords people the chance to take part **in diverse and rich cultural activities.**

Prepositional phrase as noun:

Past the village hall is the closest supermarket.

Prepositions and adverbs

To distinguish between prepositions and adverbs, remember that prepositions, unlike adverbs, can never function alone within a sentence. A preposition is always part of a prepositional phrase.

EXAMPLES:

Preposition:

The children went **into the house.**

Adverb:

They went **in.**

Preposition:

Crowds of people were skiing **down the icy slopes.**

Adverb:

After the fifth book fell **down,** we decided it was time to rearrange the bookshelves.

Prepositional idioms

Many prepositional phrases are idiomatic; there is no logical reason why one expression is accepted and another not. Since they are not governed by rules, idioms are especially difficult to learn.

Following is a representative listing of some commonly used prepositional idioms. As formal and informal writing vary, so does the use of these idioms. Refer to Section II, "Basic Glossary of Usage," and a dictionary for further information.

Common prepositional idioms

abide by

I cannot *abide by* your rules.

abide in

Kelly *abides in* Kansas.

accede to

He will not *accede to* my demand.

accessory of

Janice is an *accessory of* the thief.

accessory to

Gary is an *accessory to* the deed.

accommodate to

Marty thinks it is easy to *accommodate* oneself *to* a new location.

accommodate with

She *accommodated* them *with* an upgraded car rental.

accompany by

My aunt was *accompanied by* her nurse.

accompany with

The invoice was *accompanied with* a stamped, self-addressed envelope.

accord with

In *accord with* your wishes, they will stay at the Clarion Hotel.

according to

According to Dick, the store is opening early.

accountable for

The parents were no longer *accountable for* any debts their children might incur.

accountable to

The trainee was *accountable to* her superior.

accused by

Mary was *accused by* her children of throwing out their collection of dried leaves.

accused of

She was *accused of* lying about it, too.

acquit with

The soldier *acquitted* himself *with* dignity.

adapt from

Janet *adapted* the dress *from* a magazine picture.

adapt to

Some found it hard to *adapt to* city living.

adequate for

The land was not *adequate for* their needs.

adequate to

Their training was *adequate to* the requirements.

averse to

She was not *averse to* long hours.

advise of

The patient was *advised of* the risks the surgery entailed.

agree in

The governing board *agreed in* principle with the board's recommendations.

agree on

They cannot *agree on* what toppings to get on the pizza.

agree to

They finally *agreed to* sausage, mushroom, and meatball.

agree with

I do not *agree with* Marcia.

angry with

My dog is *angry with* me.

capable of

The child was not *capable of* lifting the heavy box.

charge for

I was *charged for* the coat.

charge with

She was *charged with* manslaughter.

commensurate with

Her raise was *commensurate with* her achievements.

compare to

You can't *compare* a man *to* a mountain.

compare with

How do these oranges *compare with* those?

comply with

They had to *comply with* the directive.

concur in

They *concurred in* urging a veto of the bill.

concur with

His anniversary *concurred with* his birthday.

conform to

Many people feel compelled to *conform to* community norms.

consist in

Vincent's worth *consists in* his skill at negotiating difficult contracts.

consist of

The handout *consists of* suggestions for community fund-raisers.

contend for

The sprinters *contended for* the blue ribbon.

correspond to

Your account *corresponds to* what we have already heard.

correspond with

I have been *corresponding with* my best friend for five years.

demand from

What did your neighbor *demand from* you in return?

demand of

She *demanded* a full account *of* the scandal.

differ over

They *differ over* ways to increase revenue.

differ with

I have always *differed with* Paul over environmental issues.

eligible for

He was *eligible for* a promotion.

excepted from

The salary is *excepted from* further deductions.

excluded from

The children were *excluded from* further evenings out.

familiar to

Your face is *familiar to* me.

familiar with

She was *familiar with* the procedure.

find for

The judge *found for* the plaintiff.

furnish with

I *furnished* them *with* my letters of recommendation.

identical to

She is *identical to* her twin.

ignorant of

They were *ignorant of* their responsibilities.

impatient at

The mother was *impatient at* her son's behavior.

impatient with

The mother was *impatient with* her son.

inconsistent in

My mother is *inconsistent in* her political views.

inconsistent with

This directive is *inconsistent with* union policy.

independent of

The bank is now *independent of* the federal system.

inferior to

This product is *inferior to* that one.

influence over

The mother had a strong *influence over* her child.

inform of

I wish people would keep me *informed of* the latest plans.

inherent in

The capacity for change is *inherent in* all.

liable for

Homeowners are *liable for* injuries visitors sustain on their property.

liberal in

Linda is *liberal in* her outlook.

liberal with

She is also very *liberal with* criticism.

necessity for

There is no *necessity for* violence.

necessity of

We are dealing with the *necessity of* cutting back on expenses.

oblivious of/to

Harry was *oblivious to* his surroundings.

part from

The mother was *parted from* her children.

part with

Lisa *parted with* her stuffed dogs.

precedent for

What is the *precedent for* this directive?

prior to

Prior to the meeting, I am going to get a cup of coffee.

reconcile to

Joel is *reconciled to* the truth.

reconcile with

I cannot *reconcile* my attitude *with* his.

rewarded for

She was *rewarded for* her perfect attendance.

rewarded with

She was *rewarded with* a lovely present.

similarity in

Is there any *similarity in* their backgrounds?

superior to

Crestwood Manor is *superior to* Greenwood Trails.

talk of

The lecturer *talked of* her experiences.

talk with

I *talked with* her after the presentation.

transfer from

Rick was *transferred from* his previous job.

transfer to

He was *transferred to* a new office.

unequal in

The children were *unequal in* height.

unequal to

Beth was *unequal to* the requirements of the new position.

use for

We have no *use for* the old drapes.

use of

We made good *use of* them anyway.

wait at

Kim was *waiting at* the information booth.

wait for

She was *waiting for* me.

wait on

The clerk *waited on* me.

Conjunctions

A conjunction is a word used to connect words, phrases, or clauses.

The three main kinds of conjunctions are **coordinating**, **correlative**, and **subordinating**. Adverbs can also be used to link related ideas. When adverbs are used in this way, they are called **conjunctive adverbs.**

Coordinating conjunctions

A coordinating conjunction is a word that functions individually to connect sentence parts.

To "coordinate" implies ranking equal ideas: Medical insurance is expensive, *but* dental insurance is prohibitive.

Coordinating conjunctions

and	but	nor	or
for	so	yet	

HOW TO USE COORDINATING CONJUNCTIONS

As a general rule, use *and, but, nor,* or *or* to connect matching words, phrases, or clauses; use *for* or *so* to connect subordinate or independent clauses rather than individual words.

The conjunctions have different meanings as well: *and* shows connection, *but, nor,* and *yet* show contrast, *or* shows choice, *so* indicates result, and *for* shows causality.

EXAMPLES:

And *shows connection:*

The children cleaned up quickly **and** quietly.

But, nor, *and* **yet** *show contrast:*

The living room was extremely elegant **but** surprisingly comfortable.

My supervisor will never give us half days on Friday, **nor** will she agree to your other demands.

She took good care of the houseplant, **yet** it wilted and lost its leaves anyway.

Or *shows choice:*

You can have the spaghetti and meatballs **or** the veal and peppers.

So *shows result:*

We missed the dinner party, **so** we ended up eating peanut butter and jelly sandwiches.

For *shows causality:*

Laura stayed in the office late all week, **for** she had to finish the project by Friday.

Correlative conjunctions

Correlative conjunctions always work in pairs to connect words, phrases, or clauses.

both . . . and	either . . . or
neither . . . nor	not only . . . but also
whether . . . or	not . . . but

EXAMPLES:

Both the bank **and** the post office are closed on national holidays.

The envelopes are **neither** in the drawer **nor** in the cabinet.

Whether you agree to implement my plan **or** not, you have to concede that it has merit.

Either you agree to ratify our contract now, **or** we will have to once again return to the bargaining table.

Not only the children **but also** the adults were captivated by the dancing bears at the circus.

Not the renters **but** the homeowners were most deeply affected by the recent change in tax laws.

Subordinating conjunctions

A subordinating conjunction is a word that connects two thoughts by making one subordinate to the other.

To ''subordinate'' suggests making one statement less important than the other: *Al-*

though some people tried to repair the tennis courts, they were unable to gain sufficient public backing. The main idea, "they were unable to gain sufficient public backing," can stand alone because it is an **independent clause** (complete sentence); the subordinate idea, "Although some people tried to repair the tennis courts," cannot stand alone because it is a **dependent clause** (sentence fragment). Either clause may come first in the sentence.

Common Subordinating Conjunctions

after	although	as
as if	as long as	as soon as
as though	because	before
even if	even though	if
if only	in order that	now that
once	rather than	since
so that	than	that
though	till	unless
until	when	whenever
where	whereas	wherever
while		

In general, subordinating conjunctions can be used in the following instances:

To show condition	To show intent	To show identification
though	that	where
as if	in order that	that

even though	so that	when
although		who
if		which
since		
provided		
less		

To show time	*To show cause*
when	because
while	since
since	
until	
after	
before	

EXAMPLES:

Subordinate clause first:

Until you make up your mind, we won't be able to leave.

Although traffic was light every morning, the employee was unable to arrive at work on time.

Independent clause first:

The little girl overheard her parents arguing in the next room even though they were whispering.

Please retype this letter after you return from lunch.

SUBORDINATING CONJUNCTIONS VERSUS PREPOSITIONS

A word such as *until, before, since, till,* or *after* can function as either a preposition or a subordinating conjunction, depending on its position in a sentence. Recall that subordinating conjunctions, unlike prepositions, connect two complete ideas.

EXAMPLES:

Subordinating conjunction:

Since you are driving in that direction anyway, please drop this movie off at the video store.

Preposition:

Since this morning, I have had a headache.

Subordinating conjunction:

After you finish reading that book, may I borrow it?

Preposition:

After lunch, I am going shopping for a new pair of shoes.

Conjunctive adverbs

A conjunctive adverb is a word that connects complete ideas by describing their relationship to each other.

Common Conjunctive Adverbs

accordingly	again	also
anyway	beside	certainly
consequently	finally	for example
further	furthermore	hence
however	incidentally	indeed
instead	likewise	meanwhile
moreover	namely	nevertheless
next	nonetheless	now
on the other hand	otherwise	similarly
still	then	thereafter
therefore	thus	undoubtedly

EXAMPLES:

The train is in very bad disrepair; **for example,** the air conditioning rarely works, the windows won't open, and the seats are broken.

The memo required an immediate response; **consequently,** we sent a fax.

You should not be angry at them for arriving early; **undoubtedly,** they were nervous and overestimated the time that the drive would take.

Conjunctive adverbs are also known as **transitions** because they link related ideas. You can distinguish conjunctive adverbs from coordinating and subordinating conjunctions easily by remembering that conjunctive adverbs can be moved within a sentence; conjunctions cannot.

EXAMPLES:

The taxi was late; **however,** we arrived in time to catch the entire first act.

The taxi was late; we arrived, **however,** in time to catch the entire first act.

The taxi was late; we arrived in time to catch the entire first act, **however.**

Although some versions are better, notice that the sentence makes sense regardless of the position of the conjunctive adverb. The same is not true with coordinating and subordinating conjunctions.

Interjections

An interjection is a word used to express strong emotion. It functions independently within a sentence.

In Latin, the word "interjection" means "something thrown in." In a sense, interjections are "thrown in" to add strong feeling. Interjections should be used sparingly in your writing. Since they are independent from the rest of the sentence, they can be set off by commas or punctuated as independent clauses.

Common Interjections

Ouch	Wow	Ah
Bah	Nonsense	Bravo
Shh	Well	Hey
Oh	Darn	Alas

EXAMPLES:

Darn! That cat got out again.

Oh! I didn't expect you to arrive this early.

Hey! Do you know what you're doing?

There are a number of other words that are used alone in a sentence. These include *please*, *thank you*, *yes*, *no*, *hello*, and *good-bye*. They are punctuated like interjections.

Phrases and Clauses

Phrases

A phrase is a group of related words that does not contain a subject and a verb.

EXAMPLES:

by the river
giving the speech
to win the game
near the pond
leaving this town
their day finished

Phrases can be used as nouns, adjectives, or adverbs. They are often classified as **prepositional** (adjectival and adverbial), **appositive,** or **verbal** (participial, gerund, and infinitive).

Types of Phrases

PREPOSITIONAL PHRASES

A prepositional phrase is a group of words that opens with a preposition and ends with a noun or pronoun.

Prepositional phrases can function as adjectives, adverbs, or nouns.

Adjectival phrases are prepositional phrases that describe a noun or pronoun. They function as adjectives to add color and description to writing.

EXAMPLES:

The price **of the dinner** was exorbitant.

My house is the one **between the twisted oak tree and the graceful weeping willow.**

Adverbial phrases are prepositional phrases that describe a verb, adjective, or adverb. They function as adverbs within a sentence.

EXAMPLES:

The joggers ran **with determination.**

My plane is scheduled to depart **at 6 P.M.**

APPOSITIVE PHRASES

An appositive phrase identifies or explains nouns and pronouns.

Nonrestrictive appositive phrases, those not necessary for the meaning of the sentence, are set off by commas. **Restrictive** appositive phrases are not set off from the sentence.

EXAMPLES:

Nonrestrictive:

The guest of honor was Dr. Brown, **a noted humanitarian.**

Michael, **a former track star,** keeps in shape by running fifty miles a week.

VERBALS

A verbal is a verb form used as another part of speech.

The verbal and all the words related to it are called a **verbal phrase.**

Participial phrases function as adjectives. They can be placed before or after the word they describe.

EXAMPLES:

Shaking with fear, the defendant stood before the jury.

She got a hamburger **drenched in mustard.**

Gerund phrases function as nouns. Gerunds always end in *-ing.*

EXAMPLES:

Swimming vigorously three times a week helps a person stay in shape.

Getting bumped from an airplane can be an expensive experience.

Infinitive phrases can function as nouns, adjectives, or adverbs. An infinitive phrase always begins with the word *to.*

EXAMPLES:

To shop in that store is a true nightmare.

The boss left them no choice but **to defy his direct orders.**

Clauses

A clause is a group of related words that contains a subject and a verb.

There are two types of clauses: **independent** (main) and **dependent** (subordinate).

An independent (main) clause can stand alone as a complete sentence. A dependent (subordinate) clause cannot stand alone as a complete sentence.

EXAMPLES:

Independent:

We swim.

He missed his train.

The little boy picked up his spaghetti carefully.

Dependent:

Swimming, **which is very good exercise,** is suitable for people of all ages.

Because he overslept, he missed his train.

Marcia, **who won the blue ribbon in the annual cooking contest,** plans to open a catering business.

Functions of dependent clauses

As with phrases, dependent clauses fulfill different functions within sentences. They can be classified as **adjectival** (relative), **adverbial, noun,** and **elliptical.**

ADJECTIVAL CLAUSES

An adjectival clause is a subordinate clause that describes a noun or pronoun.

An adjectival clause usually begins with one of the **relative pronouns:** *which, what, whatever, who, whose, whom, whoever, whomever,* or *that.* It may also begin with a **relative adverb:** *when, where, before, since,* or *why..* "Relative" means that the adverb "relates" a clause to the word it describes.

Adjectival clauses act as adjectives to add detail and description to writing. The relative pronouns act like subordinating conjunctions to connect one clause to another. But unlike subordinating conjunctions, relative pronouns are often subjects or objects within their clauses. A particular clause is identified by its function within a sentence.

In general, place an adjectival clause as close as possible to the word it describes to avoid confusion.

EXAMPLES:

Adjectival clauses beginning with a relative pronoun:

My husband and I hired those **who came with the strongest recommendations.**

The child **whom you saw in the magazine** is my youngest sister.

Adjectival clauses beginning with a relative adverb:

Did Fred tell you the reason **why he was late for work this morning**?

I remember **when my sister was a baby**.

ADVERBIAL CLAUSES

An adverbial clause is a subordinate clause that describes a verb, adjective, adverb, or verbal. Since adjectival clauses function as adverbs, these clauses tell "why," "how," "where," "when," "in what manner," "to what extent," "under what condition," or "with what result."

Adverbial clauses always begin with a subordinating conjunction. Common subordinating conjunctions include: *as, as if, as soon as, as though, because, before, even if, even though, if, if only, in order that, now that, once, rather than,* etc. Refer to page 95 for a complete list of common subordinating conjunctions.

Unlike adjectival clauses, adverbial clauses can be separated from the word they describe. Adverbial clauses can be placed at the beginning, middle, or end of a sentence. If the clause is placed at the beginning or middle of a sentence, it is often set off by commas.

Since the guests were so convivial, I soon forgot my troubles.

Did you visit the Statue of Liberty **when you were in New York?**

I decided, **after I lost an especially important file,** to make two backup copies of key documents.

NOUN CLAUSES

A noun clause is a subordinate clause that acts as a noun.

Noun clauses can function as subjects, objects, and complements within sentences. They begin either with a relative pronoun or with a word such as *how, why, where, when, if,* or *whether.*

Noun clauses can be difficult to identify. Since so many different words can be used to begin a noun clause, the opening word itself cannot be used as a determinant. You must discover the function of the clause within the sentence to identify it as a noun clause.

EXAMPLES:

What the writer said dismayed the critics.

Whoever finishes dinner first will be allowed to pick the television show.

They talked about **whether they could take the time off from work.**

ELLIPTICAL CLAUSES

An elliptical clause is a subordinate clause that is grammatically incomplete but nonetheless clear because the missing element can be understood from the rest of the sentence.

The word "elliptical" comes from "ellipsis," which means "omission." The verb from the second part of the comparison may be missing, or the relative pronouns *that, which,* and *whom* may be omitted from adjective clauses. Often these clauses begin with *as* or *than,* although any subordinate conjunction that makes logical sense can be used. In the following examples, the omitted words are supplied in parentheses.

EXAMPLES:

Chad's younger cousin is as tall **as he** (is).

Aruba is among the islands (that) **they visited on their recent cruise.**

When (he was) **only a child,** Barry was taken on a tour around the world.

Although (they were) **common fifty years ago,** passenger pigeons are extinct today.

Sentences

Parts of a sentence

A sentence is the expression of a complete thought.

There are two basic parts to every sentence: the **subject** and the **predicate.** The **simple subject** is the noun or pronoun that identifies the person, place, or thing the sentence is about. The **complete subject** is the simple subject and all the words that describe it. The **predicate** contains the verb that explains what the subject is doing. The **simple predicate** contains only the verb; the **complete predicate** contains the verb and any complements and modifiers.

EXAMPLES:

Subject
The motorcycle

Predicate
veered away from the boulder.

Subject
The new computer

Predicate
used the MS/DOS operating system.

Subject
One of Hawthorne's direct blood relatives

Predicate
was the famous "hanging judge" of the Salem witchcraft trials.

Subject
Farmingdale, in the town of Oyster Bay,

Predicate
has recently begun a massive recycling project.

Hard-to-locate subjects

COMMANDS OR DIRECTIONS

In some instances, the subject can be difficult to locate. In commands or directions, for instance, the subject is often not stated, because it is understood to be *you*.

Subject
(you)

Predicate
Please unload the dishwasher and vacuum the basement.

Subject
(you)

Predicate
Just tell me what happened that evening.

QUESTIONS

In questions, too, subjects can be difficult to locate because they often follow the verb rather than come before it. Rewriting the question as a statement will make it easier to find the subject. In the rewritten statements, the subject is in italics.

Question
Are *you* planning to go to Oregon this weekend or next?

Rewritten as a statement
You are planning to go to Oregon this weekend or next.

Question
When do you think the *report* will be ready for distribution?

Rewritten as a statement
The *report* will be ready for distribution when.

SENTENCES BEGINNING WITH "THERE" OR "HERE"

Sentences that begin with "there" or "here" do not usually open with a subject. Rephrase the sentence if you cannot locate the subject. In the following examples, the subjects are in italics in the rewritten sentences.

there *or* **here**
There is your wallet on the table.

Rewritten sentence
Your *wallet* is there on the table.

there *or* **here**
Here is the sherbet from the dairy.

Rewritten sentence
The *sherbet* from the dairy is here.

INVERTED SENTENCES

Inverted sentences place the subject after the verb for emphasis: High on the mountain over-

looking the ocean was the diver. *The diver* is
the subject; the rest, the predicate.

Sentence complements

Along with a verb, complete predicates often
contain a **complement**.

**A complement is a word or word group
that completes the meaning of the predicate.**

There are five primary kinds of sentence
complements: **direct objects, indirect objects, object complements, predicate
nominatives,** and **predicate adjectives.**
The last two are often called **subject complements.**

DIRECT OBJECTS

**A direct object is the noun, pronoun,
or word acting as a noun that completes
the meaning of a transitive verb.**

A direct object completes the meaning of the
transitive verb by receiving the action. (Intransitive action verbs do not have direct objects.) To help decide if a word is a direct
object, ask *What?* or *Whom?* after an action
verb.

Martha won the stuffed dog.
(What did she win? The stuffed dog.)

The hurricane damaged the trees and sidewalks.
(What did the hurricane damage? The trees and sidewalks.)

The waiter served Jack.
(Whom did the waiter serve? He served Jack.)

INDIRECT OBJECTS

An indirect objects is a noun or pronoun that names the person or thing that something is done to or given to.

Indirect objects are located after the action verb and before the direct object. Obviously, they are found only in sentences that have direct objects. Indirect objects answer the questions ''To whom?'' ''For whom?'' ''To what?'' or ''For what?''

EXAMPLES:

The assistant **gave** the **supervisor** the file folders.

The receptionist **handed** the **mother** the invoice.

Has the fire marshal **told you** about the new fire safety regulations?

OBJECT COMPLEMENTS

An object complement is a noun or adjective immediately after a direct object that either renames or describes it.

Object complements are found only in sentences that have direct objects.

EXAMPLES:

The scientists called the first duckbilled platypus a **hoax.**

Upon closer examination, they decided that it was a **reptile.**

SUBJECT COMPLEMENTS: PREDICATE NOMINATIVES AND PREDICATE ADJECTIVES

The word ''predicate'' indicates that subject complements, as with object complements, are found in the sentence predicates.

A subject complement is a noun, pronoun, or adjective that follows a linking verb and gives further information about the subject of a sentence.

PREDICATE NOMINATIVES

A predicate nominative is a noun or pronoun that follows a linking verb to explain the subject of a sentence.

EXAMPLES:

The new head of the division will be **Henry**.

Which of those two movies seems the better **one** to see?

PREDICATE ADJECTIVES

A predicate adjective is an adjective that follows a linking verb to explain the subject of a sentence.

EXAMPLES:

The vegetable soup smelled **delicious**.

My husband's collection of comic books grows **larger** and **more valuable** every day.

Forming sentences

Independent and dependent clauses can be combined in various ways to create four basic types of sentences: **simple, compound, complex,** and **compound-complex.**

Simple sentences

A simple sentence is one independent clause, a group of words containing a subject and a predicate.

This does not mean, however, that a simple sentence must be short. Both the subject and the verb may be compounded. In addition, a simple sentence may contain describing phrases. By definition, though, a simple sentence cannot have a subordinate clause or another independent clause.

EXAMPLES:

Single subject and verb:

Heather **shopped.**
   s   v

Compound subject:

The **carpenter** and the **electrician**
      s   s

arrived simultaneously.

Compound verb:

The shingle **flapped, folded,** and **broke**
            v   v   v

off.

Compound subject and compound verb:

Either **my mother** or **my great-aunt**
          s   s

bought and **wrapped** this lovely crystal
   v   v

decanter.

Phrases and modifiers:

Freezing unexpectedly, the **water**
                            s

in the copper lines **burst** the gaskets.
                       v

Compound sentences

A compound sentence is two or more independent clauses joined together.

Since the clauses in a compound sentence are independent, each can be written as an individual sentence. A compound sentence cannot have dependent clauses. The independent clauses can be connected by a comma and a coordinating conjunction (*and, but, or, for, so, yet*) or by a semicolon. If the clauses are very short, the comma before the coordinating conjunction is often omitted.

EXAMPLES:

Mary Jones went to the store, **but** Bill
Jones stayed home with the baby.

You may mail the enclosed form back to
our central office, **or** you may call our
customer service representative at the
number listed above.

Eddie typed the report in three hours; it
took him four hours to correct his errors.

Complex sentences

A complex sentence contains one independent clause and one or more subordinate clauses.

To distinguish it from the other clauses, the
independent clause in a complex sentence is
called the **main clause.** In a complex sentence, each clause has its own subject and
verb. The subject in the main clause is called
the **subject of the sentence;** the verb in the
main clause is called the **main verb.** An independent clause can stand alone as a complete
sentence; a dependent clause cannot.

EXAMPLES:

*As we were looking over your sign-in sheets
for May and June,*

we noticed a number of minor problems.
main clause

While Mary went to the store, Bill stayed
               subordinate clause
with the baby.
main clause

No one responded
  main clause
when she rang the front doorbell.
       subordinate clause

The owners of the small mountain inns
rejoiced   main clause
as the snow fell.
subordinate clause

Compound-complex sentences

A compound-complex sentence has at least two independent clauses and at least one dependent clause.

The compound-complex sentence is so named because it shares the characteristics of both compound and the complex sentences. As with the compound sentence, the compound-complex has at least two main clauses. As with the complex sentence, it has at least one subordinate clause. The subordinate clause can be part of an independent clause.

EXAMPLES:

*Since my memo seems to outline our
requirements fully,*
        subordinate clause
we are circulating it to all the departments;

        main clause
*please notify us if we can be of any further
assistance.*   main clause

When the heat comes,
   subordinate clause
the lakes dry up
   main clause
and farmers know that crops will fail.
        main clause

The length of a sentence has no bearing on its type; simple sentences can be longer than complex ones. Neither is one type "better" than any other: do not assume that a complex sentence is superior to a simple or compound sentence because it may be "harder." As a general rule, suit the sentence to the subject.

Review of sentence forms

The following five sentence forms are the basic templates on which all English sentences are built—no matter how complex. Note that the variations occur in the predicate section of each pattern, while the subject portion remains the same.

1. *subject + intransitive verb*
   Bond prices fell.
       s + v

2. *subject + transitive verb + direct object*
   Bob hummed the song.
       s + v +   do

3. *subject + transitive verb + direct object +
   objective complement*
   The committee appointed Eve secretary.
       s   +   v + do + oc

4. *subject + linking verb + subject complement*
   The procedure was tedious.
       s   +   v + sc

5. *subject + transitive verb + indirect object
   + direct object*
   The clerk gave us the receipt.
       s + v + io + do

Sentence function

In addition to the form they take, sentences can also be classified according to function. There are four main types of sentences: **declarative, interrogative, imperative,** and **exclamatory.**

Declarative sentences

A declarative sentence makes a statement.

EXAMPLES:

On Thursday we are going to see a movie.

We have been waiting for the movie to open for six weeks.

The reviews were excellent.

Since it makes a statement, a declarative sentence always ends with a period.

Interrogative sentences

An interrogative sentence asks a question.

Are we going to see the movie on
Tuesday?

How long have you been waiting for the
movie to open?

What did the reviewers say about it?

Since it asks a question, an interrogative
sentences always ends with a question mark.

Imperative sentences

**An imperative sentence makes a com-
mand.**

In many instances, the subject of an imperative sentence is understood to be *you* and is
thus not stated. In other instances, the sentence may be phrased as a question, but does
not end with a question mark.

EXAMPLES:

Take this money in case you change your
mind.

Clean up that mess!

Will you please favor us with a reply at
your earliest convenience.

Would someone move those books to the
other shelf, please.

Exclamatory sentences

An exclamatory sentence conveys strong feeling.

Many exclamatory sentences are very strongly stated declarative sentences. Since the exclamatory sentence conveys strong emotion, it is not found much in formal writing. An exclamatory sentence ends with an exclamation point.

EXAMPLES:

They still have not called!

The dress is ruined!

Sentence errors

Sentence errors fall into three main division: parts of sentences set off as complete (**fragments**), two or more sentences incorrectly joined (**run-ons**), and sentence parts misplaced or poorly connected to the rest of the sentence (**misplaced** or **dangling modifiers**).

Fragments

A fragment is part of a sentence pre-

sented as though it were a complete sentence.

A fragment may be missing a subject or verb or both, or it may be a subordinate clause not connected to a complete sentence. Since fragments are not complete sentences, they do not express complete thoughts.

EXAMPLES:

No subject:

Ran to catch the bus.

Ate all the chocolate hidden in the drawer.

No verb:

The box sitting in the trunk.

The man walking into the room.

No subject or verb:

Feeling happy.

Acting poorly.

Subordinate clause:

When I woke him up early this morning.

If it is as pleasant as you expect today.

CORRECTING FRAGMENTS

Fragments are often created when phrases and subordinate clauses are punctuated as though they were complete sentences. Recall that phrases can never stand alone because they are groups of words that do not have subjects or verbs. To correct phrase fragments, add the information they need to be complete.

Subordinate clauses, on the other hand, do contain subjects and verbs. Like phrases, however, they do not convey complete thoughts. They are often corrected by being connected to main clauses, although they can also be completed by dropping the subordinating conjunction. Correct each fragment in the manner that makes the most logical sense within the context of the passage and your purpose.

EXAMPLES:

Phrase fragment

a big house

Corrected

A big house at the end of the block burned down last evening.
(Fragment becomes subject; predicate is added.)

My sister recently purchased a big house.
(Fragment becomes direct object; subject

and predicate added.)

She earned enough money for a big house.
(Fragment becomes object of the preposition; subject, predicate, and direct object
added.)

Did you visit his newest acquisition, a big
house?
(Fragment becomes appositive; subject,
predicate, and direct object added.)

Subordinating clause fragment

When I woke him up early this morning.

Corrected

I woke him up early this morning.
(Subordinating conjunction is dropped.)

When I woke him up early this morning, he
was far grouchier than I expected.
(Fragment is connected to a main clause.)

Subordinating clause fragment

If it is as pleasant as you expect today.

Corrected

It is as pleasant as you expect today.
(Subordinating conjunction is dropped.)

If it is as pleasant as you expect today,

maybe we will have a chance to go to the beach.
(Fragment is connected to a main clause.)

ACCEPTABLE USES OF FRAGMENTS

In the majority of instances a fragment is considered a sentence error, but in a handful of cases fragments are acceptable in written speech, as explained below.

EXAMPLES:

Exclamations:

Oh dear!

What!

Commands:

Stop!

Close the door.

Questions:

What now?

Where to?

Answers:

To Smithtown.

Home.

Transitional phrases:

One additional point.

Writers may deliberately use fragments to achieve a specific effect in their work. This technique is often used with dialogue that mimics informal speech.

Run-ons

A run-on is two complete ideas incorrectly joined.

Run-ons are generally classified as either **comma splices** or **fused sentences.**

A **comma splice** incorrectly joins two independent clauses with a comma.

A **fused sentence** runs two independent clauses together without an appropriate conjunction or mark of punctuation.

EXAMPLES:

Comma splices:

Mary walked into the room, she found a mouse on her desk.

The vest was beautiful, it had intricate embroidery.

My sister loves *The Honeymooners*, she watches it every night at 11:00.

Fused sentences:

Many people are afraid of computers they do not realize how easy it is to learn basic programming.

All the word processing programs come with built-in lessons you can learn to do basic word processing in an afternoon or less.

The on-line spell check and thesaurus are especially handy they do not take the place of a good dictionary.

CORRECTING RUN-ON SENTENCES

There are four ways to correct both comma splices and fused sentences: separate the clauses into two separate sentences, insert a comma and coordinating conjunction between clauses to create a compound sentence, insert a semicolon between clauses, or subordinate one clause to the other to create a complex sentence.

EXAMPLES:

Create two sentences:

Mary walked into the room. She found a mouse on her desk.

Many people are afraid of computers. They do not realize how easy it is to learn basic programming.

Insert comma and coordinating conjunction:

Mary walked into the room, and she found a mouse on her desk.

Many people are afraid of computers, for they do not realize how easy it is to learn basic programming.

Insert semicolon:

Mary walked into the room; she found a mouse on her desk.

Many people are afraid of computers; they do not realize how easy it is to learn basic programming.

Subordinate one clause to the other:

When Mary walked into the room, she found a mouse on her desk.

Many people are afraid of computers, since they do not realize how easy it is to learn basic programming.

Misplaced and dangling modifiers

A misplaced modifier occurs when the

modifier appears to describe the wrong word in the sentence.

A dangling modifier occurs when a modifier does not logically or grammatically describe anything in the sentence.

As a general rule, a modifier should be placed as closely as possible to the word it modifies. When a clause, phrase, or word is placed too far from the word it modifies, the sentence may fail to convey the intended meaning and might produce ambiguity or even amusement. When this occurs, the modifier is called "misplaced."

When the noun or pronoun to which a phrase or clause refers is in the wrong place or missing, an unattached—or dangling—modifier results. As with misplaced modifiers, dangling modifiers result in confusion and unintended humor. In either instance, the reader is unable to make sense of the sentence.

EXAMPLES:

Word misplaced:

To get to the ski slope we **nearly** drove five hours.
(Since the modifier "nearly" describes "five," not "drove," the sentence should read: *To get to the ski slope we drove nearly five hours.)*

Phrase misplaced:

Paul got a glimpse of the accident **in his rearview mirror**.
(Since we can assume logically that the accident did not occur in Paul's rearview mirror, the phrase "in his rearview mirror" modifies "got a glimpse of" and should be placed closer to it. The sentence should read: *In his rearview mirror, Paul got a glimpse of the accident.)*

Clause misplaced:

My sister purchased a dog for my brother **that they call Rover**.
(The clause "that they call Rover" describes the dog, not the brother. The sentence should read: *For my brother, my sister purchased a dog that they call Rover.)*

Dangling modifier:

While sailing off the coast, a great white whale was seen.
(The construction is "dangling" because the lack of a subject leaves the reader wondering who saw the whale. To correct the error, revise the sentence as follows: *While sailing off the coast, we saw a great white whale.)*

CORRECTING MISPLACED AND DANGLING MODIFIERS

Correct misplaced modifiers by placing the phrase or clause closer to the word it is suppose to describe. In some instances, you can correct dangling modifiers by rewriting the sentence to add the missing word. In other cases, expand the verbal phrases into a clause.

EXAMPLES:

Misplaced modifier

The right belongs to every person of freedom of speech.

Modifier correctly placed

The right of freedom of speech belongs to every person.

Misplaced modifier

Every guest covered with butter was served corn on the cob.

Modifier correctly placed

Every guest was served corn on the cob covered with butter.

Misplaced modifier

We saved the balloons for the children that had been left on the table.

Modifier correctly placed

We saved the balloons that had been left on the table for the children.

Dangling modifier

While reading the book, the birds on the railing caught my eye.

Modifier corrected

While I was reading the book, the birds on the railing caught my eye.

Dangling modifier

To understand the process, an up-to-date text is a must.

Modifier corrected

For you to understand the process, you must have an up-to-date text.

Dangling modifier

Being childless for so long, the baby was a welcome addition.

Modifier corrected

Since they were childless for so long, the baby was a welcome addition.

Agreement of sentence parts

Agreement is what it sounds like—matching. Specifically, agreement refers to the matching of number, person, and gender within a sentence. Subjects and verbs must match in **number** (singular or plural) and **person** (first, second, or third). Pronouns and their antecedents (the words to which they refer) must also match in **gender** (masculine, feminine, or neuter). The following chart reviews number, person, and gender.

First person
The speakers: I, we

Number

Singular	Plural
I am here.	*We* are here.
I was here.	*We* were here.
I begin.	*We* begin.

Second person:
Those spoken to: you

Number

Singular	Plural
You are here	You are here.
You were here.	You were here.

Third person:
Those spoken about: he, she, it, they

Number

Singular	Plural
He (She) is here.	They are here.
It is here	
She (He) was here.	They were here.
It was here.	

Gender
Masculine

Nouns that name males

Pronouns referring to males: he, him

Feminine

Nouns that name females

Pronouns referring to females: she, her

Neuter

Nouns that name ideas, places, things, qualities

Pronouns referring to the above list: it

Sentences that do not maintain agreement among all their elements sound clumsy; they can be ambiguous as well. Sentences in which all the parts do agree help make your point more clearly and logically. There are several situations that can cause difficulty with agreement.

A subject must agree with its verb in number.

A singular subject takes a singular verb. A plural subject takes a plural verb.

Locate the subject

First, find the subject; then determine whether it is singular or plural. The subject is the noun or pronoun that is doing the action. Often, it will be located at the beginning of the sentence, as in the following example: *I* recommend that company highly. Here, the subject *I* is doing the action *recommend*.

Sometimes the subject will follow the verb, as in questions and in sentences beginning with *here* and *there*. In the following example, the verb *are* comes before the subject, *roads:* There *are* two *roads* you can use. The same is true of the placement of subject and verb in the following question, as the verb *is* comes before the subject briefcase: Where *is* your *briefcase?*

Determine if the subject is singular or plural

After you have located the subject, decide whether it is singular or plural. In English, confusion arises because most present-tense **verbs** (with the notable exceptions of *be* and *have*) add *-s* or *-es* when their subject is third-person singular (He *runs* fast; She *eats* a lot), while **nouns** ending in *-s* or *-es* are plural (potatoes, computers). The following chart shows how regular English verbs are conjugated in the present tense:

Singular	*Plural*
I dream	we dream
you dream	you dream
he (she, it) dreams	they dream

There are a number of plural nouns that are regarded as singular in meaning, as well as other nouns that can be both singular and plural, depending on the context of the sentence. *Athletics, economics, news, measles, politics, physics,* and *statistics,* for example, are often treated as singular nouns. *Mathematics,* on the other hand, can idiomatically be used with either a singular or a plural verb. Consult Section II, "Basic Glossary of Usage," or a dictionary for additional examples.

EXAMPLES:

There **are** many different **views** on the subject.

A **case** of folders **is** on sale today.

Margie works long hours in her new job.

Words that intervene between a subject and a verb do not affect subject-verb agreement.

Often, a phrase or clause will intervene between a subject and a verb. These intervening words do not affect subject-verb agreement, as illustrated in the following examples.

EXAMPLES:

The **supervisor** of the department, together with his sales force, **is** taking the late-afternoon shuttle.

The **representatives** for the congressman **are** exploring alternate methods of disposing of newspapers.

A **display** of luscious foods sometimes **encourages** impulse buying.

The **profits** earned this quarter **are** much higher than we had expected.

In general, singular subjects connected by or, nor, either . . . or, or neither . . . nor take a singular verb if both subjects are singular, a plural verb if both subjects are plural.

In the following example the singular verb *has* is used since both *supervisor* and *colleague* are singular: Either your *supervisor* or your *colleague has* to take responsibility for the error. In the next example the plural verb *have* is used since both *supervisors* and *colleagues* are plural: Either *supervisors* or *colleagues have* to take responsibility for the error.

EXAMPLES:

Neither the **sled** nor the **snow shovel has** been put away.

Either the **clown** or the **magician is** scheduled to appear at the library this Sunday afternoon.

Neither **boots** nor **shoes are** included in the one-day sale.

If a subject consists of both singular and plural nouns or pronouns connected by *or* or *nor,* the verb usually agrees with the nearer noun or pronoun.

In the following sentence, the plural verb *have* agrees with the plural noun *members:* Neither the *mayor* nor the council *members* have yielded. Notice how the verb becomes singular when *mayor* and *members* switch order: Neither the council *members* nor the *mayor* has yielded. Practice in this matter varies, however, and often the presence of one plural subject, no matter what its position, results in the use of a plural verb. Sometimes writers will place the plural subject closest to the verb to avoid awkwardness.

EXAMPLES:

Neither **we** nor **she has** distributed the memo yet.

Neither **she** nor **we have** distributed the memo yet.

Either **Martha, Ruth,** or the **Champney girls are** planning to organize the sweet sixteen party.

Two or more subjects, phrases, or clauses connected by *and* take a plural verb.

Whether the individual subjects are singular or plural, together they form a compound subject, which is plural.

EXAMPLES:

The **president** and his **advisors were** behind schedule.

The **faculty** and **staff have** planned a joint professional retreat.

Richard and his **dog jog** before work every morning.

Sleeping late Sunday morning and **reading** the paper leisurely **help** relax me after a long week at work.

Traditionally, when the subjects joined by *and* refer to the same object or person or stand for a single idea, the entire subject is treated as a unit. Most often, the personal pronoun or article before the parts of the compound subject indicates whether the subject is indeed seen as a unit. As with other matters of agreement, this varies widely in actual use.

EXAMPLES:

Unit as singular:
Ham and swiss is my favorite sandwich.

My **mentor and friend guides** me through difficult career decisions. (mentor and friend as the same person)

Unit as plural:
Ham and **swiss make** a great sandwich.

My **mentor** and my **friend guide** me through difficult career decisions. (mentor and friend are two different people)

Mixed units:
Ham and eggs was once considered a nutritious and healthful breakfast; now, **oat bran** and **fresh fruit are** considered preferable.

Nouns that refer to weight, extent, time, fractions, portions, or amount *considered as one unit* usually take a singular verb; those that indicate *separate units* usually take a plural verb.

In the first two examples below, the subjects are considered as single units and thus take a singular verb. In the last two, the subjects are considered as individual items and thus take a plural verb.

EXAMPLES:

Seventy-five cents is more than enough to buy what you want at the penny carnival.

Three fourths of the harvest **was** saved through their heroic efforts.

Half of the nails **were** rusted.

Fifty pounds of fresh chicken **are** being divided among the eager shoppers.

Collective nouns

Collective nouns (words that are singular in form but refer to a group) may be either singular or plural, depending on the meaning of the sentence.

Collective nouns have a singular form but identify a group of people or objects. When a collective noun is used as the subject of a sentence, it can be singular or plural, depending on the context.

Collective nouns that are usually considered singular

acoustics	army	assembly
association	athletics	audience
board	cabinet	class
commission	committee	company
corporation	council	counsel

couple	crowd	department
family	firm	goods
group	gymnastics	half
headquarters	herd	jury
legion	majority	minority
navy	number	pair
part	percent	platoon
politics	press	public
remainder	series	staff
statistics	tactics	United States

Collective nouns that are usually considered plural

assets	earnings	goods
headquarters	means	odds
pincers	pliers	premises
proceeds	quarters	savings
scissors	tidings	trousers
wages	winnings	whereabouts

Although plural in form, nouns such as *measles, blues, mumps,* and *economics* usually take a singular verb. The phrase *the number* is almost always singular, but the phrase *a number* is almost always plural. The title of a book, even when plural in form, usually takes a singular verb. The names of companies can be singular or plural. Usually, those that end with a singular sound are treated as singular; those that end with a plural sound, plural.

Determine agreement for each collective noun on a sentence-by-sentence basis. If the sentence implies that the group named by the collective noun acts as a single unit, use a singular verb. If the sentence implies that the group named by the collective noun acts individually, use a plural verb.

COLLECTIVE NOUNS AS SINGULAR

Collective nouns are usually treated as singular when the members of the group act, or are considered, as a unit.

EXAMPLES:

The budget **committee is** evaluating expenditures this week.

The **team has** five games scheduled for September alone.

The **jury,** not the judge, **makes** the final decision.

Measles is extremely contagious.

Gotthelf & Company is hosting its annual holiday party this Friday evening.

Five hundred dollars is the amount you owe.

Agreement of collective nouns is not uniform on both sides of the Atlantic, however:

standard British usage treats nouns like *legion*, *committee*, and *government* for example, as plural. Keep your intended audience in mind and double-check pronoun number in the dictionary.

Pronouns

A pronoun must agree with its antecedent—the word to which the pronoun refers—in number and gender.

Traditionally, certain indefinite pronouns were always considered singular, some were always considered plural, and some could be both singular and plural. As language changes, however, many of these rules are changing. *None*, for example, was always treated as a singular pronoun, even though it has been used with both singular and plural verbs since the ninth century. When the sense is "not any persons or things," the plural is more commonly used: The rescue party searched for survivors, but *none were* found. When *none* is clearly intended to mean *not one* or *not any*, it is followed by a singular verb: Of all my court cases, *none has* been stranger than yours.

The following lists, therefore, are presented as general guidelines, not hard-and-fast rules.

In general, use singular verbs with indefinite pronouns.

As the following chart shows, most indefinite pronouns are usually considered singular in meaning.

Indefinite pronouns that are most often considered singular

all	any	anybody
anyone	any one	anything
each	either	every
everybody	everyone	every one
everything	many a	neither
nobody	none	no one
nothing	one	somebody
someone	some one	something

Indefinite pronouns that are most often considered plural

both	few	many
others	several	

Indefinite pronouns that can be considered singular or plural

all	any	none
more	most	some

EXAMPLES:

Each of the people observes all the safety regulations.

Few are comfortable on a job interview.

Some of the water **is** seeping into the wall, but **some** of the files **remain** dry.

All the food **has** been donated to charity.

All the children **have** left to go to school together.

Sometimes even when all the elements in a sentence agree, the sentence will still sound awkward. This is especially true of plural verbs with collective nouns. If this is the case, re-write the sentence to eliminate the awkwardness.

Shifts

A shift is an unnecessary or illogical change of tense, voice, mood, person, number, tone or style, viewpoint, or direct and indirect quotations within a sentence, paragraph, or essay. While there are times when it is necessary to shift one of these elements to clarify meaning, unnecessary shifts confuse your reader and distort the meaning of your writing.

Avoid illogical and unnecessary shifts.

Shifts in tense

A shift in **tense** occurs when the tenses of verbs within a sentence or paragraph do not logically match. Sometimes, however, it is necessary to shift tenses to indicate specific changes in meaning. In the following example, the shift in tense is necessary to underscore the parallel career choices between mother and daughter by explaining that Kathy's career will occur in the future, while her mother worked in the same field in the past: Kathy *will become* a lawyer thirty years after her mother *was admitted* to the bar. But shifts in tense not required by the meaning of the sentence are distracting to your reader, as the following examples illustrate.

EXAMPLES:

Confusing:

Michigan **was** a land-grant university and therefore two years of military drill **will be** compulsory.

Revised:

Michigan **was** a land grant university and therefore two years of military drill **was** compulsory.

Confusing:

Throughout the eighties the junk bond market **rose** steadily; as a result, small investors **invest** heavily from 1985 to 1989.

Revised:

Throughout the eighties the junk bond market **rose** steadily; as a result, small investors **invest** heavily from 1985 to 1989.

Confusing:

Last night I **was watching** my favorite television show. Suddenly the show **is interrupted** for a special news bulletin. I **lean** forward and **will** eagerly **watch** the screen for information.

Revised:

Last night I **was watching** my favorite television show. Suddenly the show **was** interrupted for a special news bulletin. I **leaned** forward and eagerly **watched** the screen for information.

Shifts in voice

Voice shows whether the subject of the verb acts or is acted upon. When the subject of the verb does the action, the sentence is said to be in the **active voice:** I *hit* the ball across the field. When the subject of the verb receives the action, the sentence is said to be in the **passive voice:** The ball *was hit* by me.

As with shifts in tense, there are times when it will be necessary to shift voice within a sentence. Sometimes a shift in voice will help a reader zero in on the focus of the sentence, as in the following example: The volunteer *worked* diligently and *was rewarded* with a paid position in the organization. Shifts in voice also serve to give emphasis: Despite town board protests, planned repairs to the town swimming pool *were shelved* for the time being. Unnecessary shifts in voice, however, can confuse readers, as the following examples show.

EXAMPLES:

Confusing:

As **we finished** our coffee and tea, the waiters and waitresses **were seen** clearing the adjacent tables.

Revised:

As **we finished** our coffee and tea, **we saw** the waiters and waitresses clearing the adjacent tables.

Confusing:

The **cook mixed** the bread dough until it was blended and then **it was set** in the warm oven to rise.

Revised:

The **cook mixed** the bread dough until it was blended and then **set it** in the warm oven to rise.
    OR
The **bread dough was mixed** until it was

blended and then **it was set** in the warm oven to rise.

Shifts in mood

As with tense and voice, there are occasions when writers have to shift **mood** within or between sentences to make their meaning clear. Unnecessary shifts in mood, however, can cause confusion.

Shifts in mood often occur in giving directions, when a writer moves between the **imperative mood** and the **indicative mood**. Some writers feel that directions are more effective when given in the imperative mood. The following examples illustrate annoying or confusing shifts in mood:

EXAMPLES:

Confusing:

Stroke the paint on evenly, but **you should not dab it on** corners and edges. (shift from imperative to indicative)

Revised:

Stroke the paint on evenly, but **don't dab it on** corners and edges.
   OR
You should stroke the paint on evenly,

but **you shouldn't dab it on** corners and edges.

Confusing:

The cleaning service asked that **they get better hours** and **they want to work fewer weekends** as well. (shift from subjunctive to indicative)

Revised:

The cleaning service asked **that they get better hours** and **that they work fewer weekends** as well.

OR

The cleaning service asked **to work better hours** and **fewer weekends.**

OR

The cleaning service wants **to work better hours** and **fewer weekends.**

Shifts in person

Person means the form a pronoun or verb takes to show the person or persons speaking: the first person *(I, we)*, second person *(you)*, or third person *(he, she, it, they)*. As the pronouns indicate, the **first person** is the person talking, the **second person** is the person spoken to, and the **third person** is the person, concept, or thing spoken about.

Shifts between the second- and third-person

pronouns cause the most confusion. Some people feel that these shifts are the most common because English allows us to refer to people in general in both the second person *(you)* and the third person *(a person, one; people, they)*. The following examples illustrate common shifts in person and different ways to revise such shifts.

EXAMPLE:

Confusing:

When **one** shops for an automobile, **you** should research various models in consumer magazines and read all the advertisements as well as speak to salespeople. (shift from the third to the second person)

Revised:

When **you** shop for an automobile, **you** should research various models in consumer magazines and read all the advertisements as well as speak to salespeople.

   OR

When **one** shops for an automobile, **one** should research various models in consumer magazines and read all the advertisements as well as speak to salespeople.

   OR

When **people** shop for an automobile, **they** should research various models in consumer magazines and read all the advertisements as well as speak to salespeople.

Confusing:

When **a person** applies themselves diligently, **you** can accomplish a surprising amount.

Revised:

When **people** apply themselves diligently, **they** can accomplish a surprising amount.
   OR
When **you** apply yourself diligently, **you** can accomplish a surprising amount.
   OR
When **a person** applies himself or herself diligently, **he or she** can accomplish a surprising amount.

Shifts in perspective

Shifts in **perspective** are related to shifts in person in that both change the vantage point from which a piece of writing is told. As with other shifts, there will be occasions when it is desirable to shift perspective, but unnecessary shifts confuse readers. In the following example, the perspective shifts from above the water to below without adequate transition.

EXAMPLE:

Confusing:

The frothy surface of the ocean danced with bursts of light and the fish swam lazily through the clear water and waving plants.

Revised:

The frothy surface of the ocean danced with bursts of light; **below,** the fish swam lazily through the clear water and waving plants.

Shifts in number

Number indicates one (**singular**) or many (**plural**). Shifts in number occur with nouns and personal pronouns because both change form to show differences in number. Confusion with number occurs especially often between a pronoun and its antecedent and between words whose meanings relate to each other. As a general rule, shifts in number can be corrected if singular pronouns are used to refer to singular antecedents and plural pronouns are used to refer to plural antecedents. The following examples show how shifts in number can be revised for greater clarity and improved style.

EXAMPLES:

Confusing:

If **a person** does not keep up with house-hold affairs, **they** will find that things pile up with alarming speed. (shift from singular to plural)

Revised:

If **a person** does not keep up with house-hold affairs, **he or she** will find that things pile up with alarming speed.

OR

If **people** do not keep up with household affairs, **they** will find that things pile up with alarming speed.

Confusing:

All the repair **stations** have a good **reputation**. (*repair stations* is plural; *reputation* is singular)

Revised:

All the repair **stations** have good **reputations**.

Person and number with collective nouns

Maintaining consistency of person and number is especially tricky with collective nouns, since many can be either singular or plural, depending on the context. Once you establish a collective noun as singular or plural within a sentence, maintain consistency throughout.

EXAMPLES:

Confusing:

Because my **company** bases **their** bonus on amount of income generated yearly, we must all do our share to enable **it** to give a generous bonus. (*company* can be either singular or plural)

Revised:

Because my **company** bases **its** bonus on amount of income generated yearly, we must all do our share to enable **it** to give a generous bonus.
    OR
Because my **company** bases **their** bonus on amount of income generated yearly, we must all do our share to enable **them** to give a generous bonus.

Confusing:

The **jury is** divided on whether or not **they** should demand additional evidence.

Revised:

The **jury are** divided on whether or not **they**

should demand additional evidence. (*jury functioning as separate individuals*)

Shifts in tone and style

Tone in writing is the writer's attitude toward his or her readers and subject. As pitch and volume convey tone in speaking, so word choice and sentence structure help convey tone in writing. Tone can be formal or informal, humorous or earnest, distant or friendly, pompous or personal, or any number of different stances. Obviously, different tones are appropriate for different audiences.

Style is a writer's way of writing. Style comprises every way a writer uses language. Elements of style include tone, word choice, figurative language, grammatical structure, rhythm, and sentence length and organization.

Generally speaking, a piece of writing is more powerful and effective if consistent tone and style are maintained throughout. Needless shifts in tone and style confuse readers and weaken the impact of a piece of writing.

EXAMPLES:

Shift:

Reporters who assert that freedom of the

press can be maintained without judicial intervention are **really bananas.** (shift from elevated diction to colloquial)

Revised:

Reporters who assert that freedom of the press can be maintained without judicial intervention are **greatly mistaken.**

Shift:

Their leave-taking was marked by the same **cool** that had characterized their entire visit with us. Later, we discussed their good humor, consideration, and generosity. (shift from colloquial to standard written English)

Revised:

Their leave-taking was marked by the same **affability** that had characterized their entire visit with us. Later, we discussed their good humor, consideration, and generosity.

Shifts in direct and indirect quotations

Direct quotations use quotation marks to report a speaker's exact words: ''I'll be the referee for this week's game,'' Mr. Kinsella said. Usually, direct quotations are also marked by a phrase such as *she said* or *he remarked,* which indicates the speaker.

Indirect quotations report what was said, but not necessarily in the speaker's own words: Mr. Kinsella said that he would be the referee for this week's game. Since the remarks do not have to be reproduced exactly, indirect quotations do not use quotation marks. Often, a reported statement will be introduced by *that, who, how, if, what, why,* or *whether.*

Illogical shifts between direct and indirect quotations can become wordy, lead to illogical tense shifts, and confuse readers. As the following examples show, these errors can usually be eliminated by recording a speaker's remarks with logic and consistency regardless of whether direct or indirect quotations or a combination of the two are used.

EXAMPLES:

Wordy:

Poet and critic T. S. Eliot said that he feels that the progress of an artist was like a long process of sacrifice of self, "a continual extinction of personality."

Revised:

Poet and critic T. S. Eliot said that the progress of an artist is "a continual self-sacrifice, a continual extinction of personality."

OR

Poet and critic T. S. Eliot said that to progress, artists must sacrifice and extinguish the self.

Confusing:

Jill asked whether we had cut down the storm-damaged tree and ''Was there any further damage?''

Revised:

Jill asked whether we had cut down the storm-damaged tree and if there was any further damage.

OR

Jill asked, ''Have you cut down the storm-damaged tree and was there any further damage?''

Parallel Structure

Parallel structure, or **parallelism**, means that grammatical elements that share the same function will share the same form. Parallel structure ensures that ideas of equal rank are expressed in similar ways and that separate word groups appear in the same grammatical form.

Individual words, phrases, clauses, or sentences can be paralleled. For example, nouns are paired with nouns, and verbs correspond with matching verbs in tense, mood, and number. Parallel structure helps coordinate ideas and strengthen logic and symmetry.

EXAMPLES:

Words not parallel:

The child was **hot, cranky,** and **needed food.**

Parallel:

The child was **hot, cranky,** and **hungry.**

Phrases not parallel:

He has **plundered** our seas, **ravaged** our coasts, and **was burning** our towns. . . —Jefferson

Parallel:

He has **plundered** our seas, **ravaged** our coasts, **burnt** our towns . . .

Clauses not parallel:

The **only good** is knowledge, and evil is the **only ignorant thing.**—Diogenes Laertius

Parallel:

The **only good** is knowledge, and the **only evil** is ignorance.

Sentences not parallel:

Cursed be the social wants that sin against the strength of youth!
Cursed be the social ties that warp us from the living truth!
Cursed be the sickly forms that err from honest nature's rule!
The gold that gilds the straighten'd forehead of the fool **is** also **cursed.**

Parallel:

Cursed be the social wants that sin against the strength of youth!

Cursed be the social ties that warp us from
the living truth!
Cursed be the sickly forms that err from
honest nature's rule!
Cursed be the gold that gilds the straight-
en'd forehead of the fool.

Parallel items in series

Items in a series usually have greater impact
when arranged in parallel order. The items can
be words, phrases, or clauses.

EXAMPLES:

Passions, prejudices, fears, and neuroses
spring from ignorance, and take the form
of myth and illusions.—Sir Isaiah Berlin

When any of the four pillars of the
government, religion, justice, counsel, and
treasure, are mainly shaken or weakened,
men have need to pray for fair weather.
—Francis Bacon

Parallel items in pairs

In the opening of *A Tale of Two Cities*, Charles
Dickens arranged paired items in a series for
a powerful effect:

It was the best of times, it was the worst of times,

it was the age of wisdom, it was the age of foolishness,

it was the epoch of belief, it was the epoch of incredulity,

it was the season of Light, it was the season of Darkness,

it was the spring of hope, it was the winter of despair . . .

Coordinating and correlative conjunctions

Use coordinating and correlative conjunctions to establish parallelism.

Parallel structure is especially effective with coordinating conjunctions *(and, but, or, nor, so, for, yet)* and correlative conjunctions *(both . . . and; either . . . or; neither . . . nor; not only . . . but also; whether . . . or).*

Coordinating conjunctions

EXAMPLES:

Not parallel:

The homemaker was **organized, efficient,** and **a hard worker.**

Parallel:

The homemaker was **organized, efficient, and hardworking.**

Not parallel:

Knowing how to win is important, but it is even more important **to know** how to lose.

Parallel:

Knowing how to win is important, but **knowing** how to lose is even more important.

Not parallel:

We can **go out** to eat, or **ordering in** a pizza would do as well.

Parallel:

We can **go out** to eat, or we can **order in** a pizza.

Correlative conjunctions

EXAMPLES:

Not parallel:

The hosts paid attention **not only to the refreshments,** but they **also were paying attention** to the music.

Parallel:

The hosts paid attention **not only to the refreshments but also to the music.**

Not parallel:

Either take down the screens **or you clean** the garage out.

Parallel:

Either take down the screens **or clean** out the garage.

Not parallel:

Neither the **dripping cat** nor the **dog that was muddy** was welcome in my foyer.

Parallel:

Neither the **dripping cat** nor the **muddy dog** was welcome in my foyer.

Clarify parallel construction by repeating words

In longer sentences, repeating a preposition, an article, *to* from the infinitive, or introductory words from phrases or clauses can underscore the parallelism.

EXAMPLE:

As the winter days grow shorter and colder, and **when** cabin fever sets in, I take out my travel books and dream of exotic islands.

Parallel outlines and lists

Arranging outlined ideas and lists in parallel structure helps solidify thinking. Maintaining one format (for example, complete sentences, clauses, or phrases) throughout serves to order ideas, as the following sentence outline shows.

I. Cigarette smoke harms the health of the general public.
  A. Cigarette smoke may lead to serious diseases in nonsmokers.
    1. It leads to lung cancer.
      a. It causes emphysema.
      b. It causes mouth cancer.
    2. It leads to circulatory disease.
      a. It causes strokes.
      b. It causes heart disease.
  B. Cigarette smoke worsens less serious health conditions in nonsmokers.
    1. It aggravates allergies.
    2. It intensifies pulmonary infections.

Section II

Basic Glossary of Usage

Language and the way it is used change constantly. This glossary provides a concise guide to contemporary English usage. It will show you how certain words and phrases are used and why certain usage is unacceptable.

"Informal" indicates that a word or phrase is often used in everyday speech but should generally be avoided in formal discourse. "Nonstandard" means that the word or phrase is not suitable for everyday speech and writing or in formal discourse. The "Glossary" also covers many frequently confused words and homonyms. Additional words and phrases may be checked in the *Random House Dictionary of the English Language*.

a/an In both spoken and written English, **an** is used before words beginning with a vowel sound *(He carried an umbrella. The Nobel is an honor)* and when the consonants *f, h, l, m, n, r, s,* and *x* are pronounced by name *(The renovations created an L-shaped room. Miles received an F in physics).* Use **a** before words beginning with a consonant sound *(What a fish! I bought a computer)* and words that start with vowels but are pronounced as consonants *(A union can be dissolved. They live in a one-room apartment).* Also use **a** with words that start with consonant letters not listed above and with the vowel *u (She earned a C in French. He made a U-turn).*

For words that begin with *h,* if the initial *h* is not pronounced, the word is preceded by **an** *(It will take an hour).* Adjectives such as *historic, historical, heroic,* and *habitual* are commonly preceded by **an,** especially in British English, but the use of **a** is common in both writing and speech. *(She read a historical novel).* When the *h* is strongly pronounced, as in a stressed first syllable, the word is preceded by **a** *(I bought a history of Long Island).*

above Above can be used as an adjective *(The above entry is incomplete)* or as a noun *(First, please read the above)* in referring to what has been previously mentioned in a passage. Both uses are standard in formal writing.

accept/except **Accept** is a verb meaning "to receive": *Please accept a gift.* **Except** is usually a preposition or a conjunction meaning "other than" or "but for": *He was willing to accept an apology from everyone except me.* When **except** is used as a verb, it means "to leave out": *He was excepted from the new regulations.*

accidentally/accidently The correct adverb is **accidentally**, from the root word **accidental**, not **accident** (*Russell accidentally slipped on the icy sidewalk*). **Accidently** is a misspelling.

adoptive/adopted **Adoptive** refers to the parent: *He resembles his adoptive father.* **Adopted** refers to the child: *Their adopted daughter wants to adopt a child herself.*

adverse/averse Both words are adjectives, and both mean "opposed" or "hostile." **Averse,** however, is used to describe a subject's opposition to something (*The minister was averse to the new trends developing in the country*), whereas **adverse** describes something opposed to the subject (*The adverse comments affected his self-esteem*).

advice/advise **Advice,** a noun, means "suggestion or suggestions": *Here's some good advice.* **Advise,** a verb, means "to offer ideas or suggestions": *Act as we advise you.*

affect/effect Most often, **affect** is a verb, meaning "to influence," and **effect** is a noun meaning "the result of an action": *His speech affected my mother very deeply, but had no effect on my sister at all.* **Affect** is also used as a noun in psychology and psychiatry to mean "emotion": *We can learn much about affect from performance.* In this usage, it is pronounced with the stress on the first syllable. **Effect** is also used as a verb meaning "to bring about": *His letter effected a change in their relationship.*

aggravate/annoy The informal speech and writing **aggravate** can be used as a synonym for **annoy**. However, in formal discourse the words mean different things and should be used in this way: *Her back condition was aggravated by lifting the child, but the child's crying annoyed her more than the pain.*

agree to/agree with **Agree to** means "to consent to, to accept" (usually with a plan or idea). **Agree with** means "to be in accord with" (usually with a person or group): *I can't believe they will agree to setting up a business together when they don't agree with each other on anything.*

ain't The term is nonstandard for am not, isn't, or aren't. It is used in formal speech and writing only for humorous effect, usually in dialogue.

aisle/isle Aisle means "a passageway between sections of seats": *It was impossible to pass through the airplane aisle during the meal service.* Isle means "island": *I would like to be on a desert isle on such a dreary morning.*

all/all of Use **all** to describe a noun: *I signed the letter with all my kisses.* Use **all of** before a pronoun or proper noun: *All of them will go.*

all ready/already All ready, a pronoun and an adjective, means "entirely prepared"; **already,** an adverb, means "so soon" or "previously": *I was all ready to leave when I noticed that it was already dinner time.*

all right/alright All right is always written as two words: **alright** is a misspelling: *Betsy said that it was all right to use her car that afternoon.*

allusion/illusion An **allusion** is a reference or hint: *He made an allusion to the past.* An **illusion** is a deceptive appearance: *The canals on Mars are an illusion.*

almost/most Almost, an adverb, means "nearly"; **most,** an adjective, means "the greatest part of" something. **Most** is not synonymous with **almost,** as the following example shows: *During our vacation we shop at that store almost every day and buy most of the available snack foods.*

In informal speech, **most** (as a shortened form of **almost**) is used as an adverb. It occurs before such pronouns as *all, anyone, anybody, everyone,* and *everybody;* the adjectives *all, any,* and *every;* and the adverbs *anywhere* and *everywhere.* For example: *Most everyone around here is related.* The use of **most** as an adverb is nonstandard and is uncommon in formal writing except when used to represent speech.

a lot/alot/allot A lot is always written as two words. It is used informally to mean "many": *The unrelenting heat frustrated a lot of people.* **Allot** is a verb meaning "to divide" or "to set aside": *We allot a portion of the yard for a garden.* **Alot** is not a word.

altogether/all together Altogether means "completely" or "totally"; **all together** means "all at one time" or "gathered together": *It is altogether proper that we recite the Pledge all together.*

allude/elude Both words are verbs. **Allude** means "to mention briefly or accidentally": *During our conversation, he alluded to his vacation plans.* **Elude** means "to avoid or escape": *The thief has successfully eluded capture for six months.*

altar/alter Altar is a noun meaning "a sacred place or platform": *The couple ap-*

proached the altar for the wedding ceremony.
Alter is a verb meaning "to make different; to change": *He altered his appearance by losing fifty pounds, growing a beard, and getting a new wardrobe.*

A.M., P.M./a.m., p.m. These abbreviations for time are most frequently restricted to use with figures: *The ceremony begins at 10:00 A.M. (not ten thirty in the A.M.)*

among/between **Among** is used to indicate relationships involving more than two people or things, while **between** is used to show relationships involving two people or things, or to compare one thing to a group to which it belongs: *The three quarrelled among themselves because she had to choose between two of them.* **Between** is also used to express relationships of persons or things considered individually, no matter how many: *Between holding public office, teaching, and raising a family, she has little free time.*

amount/number **Amount** refers to quantity that cannot be counted: *The amount of work accomplished before a major holiday is always negligible.* **Number,** in contrast, refers to things that can be counted: *He has held a number of jobs in the past five months.* But some concepts, like time, can use either **amount** or **number,** depending how the elements are identified in the specific sentence:

We were surprised by the amount of time it took us to settle into our new surroundings. The number of hours it took to repair the sink pleased us.

and etc. Since **etc.** means "and all the rest," **and etc.** is redundant; the "and" is not needed. Many prefer to use "and so forth" or "and the like" as a substitute for the abbreviation.

and/or The combination **and/or** is used mainly in legal and business writing. Its use should be avoided in general writing, as in *He spends his weekends watching television and/or snacking.* In such writing, either one or the other word is sufficient. If you mean either, use **or**; if you mean both, use **and**. To make a greater distinction, revise the phrasing: *He spends his weekends watching television, snacking, or both.*

and which/and who "And" is unnecessary when "which" or "who" is used to open a relative clause. Use **and which** or **and who** only to open a second clause starting with the same relative pronoun: *Elizabeth is my neighbor who goes shopping every morning and who calls me every afternoon to tell me about the sales.*

a number/the number As a subject, **a number** is most often plural and **the number** is singular: *A number of choices are available. The number of choices is limited.* As with many agreement questions, this guideline is followed more often in formal discourse than in speech and informal writing.

ante-/anti- The prefix **ante-** means "before" *(antecedent, antechamber, antediluvian)*; the prefix **anti-** means against *(antigravity, antifreeze).* **Anti-** takes a hyphen before an *i* or a capital letter: *anti-Marxist, anti-inflationary.* Consult the dictionary for exceptions.

anxious/eager Traditionally, **anxious** means "nervous" or "worried" and consequently describes negative feelings. In addition, it is usually followed by the word "about"; *I'm anxious about my exam.* **Eager** means "looking forward" or "anticipating enthusiastically" and consequently describes positive feelings. It is usually followed by "to": *I'm eager to get it over with.* Today, however, it is standard usage for **anxious** to mean "eager": *They are anxious to see their new home.*

anybody, any body/anyone, any one Anybody and anyone are pronouns; any body is a noun modified by "any" and any one is a pronoun or adjective modified by "any." They are used as follows: *Can anybody speak to any body in this office? Will anyone help me? I have more cleaning than any one person can ever do.*

any more/anymore Any more means "no more"; **anymore,** an adverb, means "now": *We don't want any more trouble. We won't go there anymore.*

anyplace Anyplace is an informal expression for "anywhere." It occurs in speech and informal writing but is best avoided in formal prose.

anyways/anyway; anywheres/anywhere Anyways is nonstandard for **anyway;** anywheres is nonstandard for **anywhere.**

apt/likely Apt is standard in all speech and writing as a synonym for "likely" in suggesting chance without inclination: *They are apt to call any moment now.* Likely, meaning "probably," is frequently preceded by a qualifying word: *The new school budget will very likely raise taxes.* However, likely without the qualifying word is standard in all varieties of English: *The new school budget will likely raise taxes.*

as Do not use as in place of *who* or *whether:* *We're not sure whether (not "as") you should do that. That's the person who (not "as") I spoke to you about.* Also avoid using as as a substitute for *because, since, while, whether, or who,* where its use may create confusion. In the following sentence, for example, as may mean "while" or "because": *As they were* *driving to California, they decided to see the Grand Canyon.*

as/because/since While all three words can function as subordinating conjunctions, they carry slightly different shades of meaning. **As** establishes a time relationship and can be used interchangeably with **when** or **while**. **Because** and **since,** in contrast, describe causes and effects: *As we brought out the food, it began to drizzle. Because (since) Nancy goes skiing infrequently, she prefers to rent skis.*

as/like **As** is a conjunction or a preposition; **like** is a preposition only. Therefore, use **as** or **as if** to introduce a full clause: *The author uses images in his poems as he does in his stories. This book is like the other one.* When **as** functions as a preposition, the distinction between **as** and **like** depends on meaning: **As** suggests that the subject is equivalent to the description: *He was employed as a teacher.* **Like,** in contrast, suggests similarity but not equivalence: *Speakers like her excel in front of large groups.*

ascent/assent **Ascent** is a noun that means "a move upward or a climb": *Their ascent up Mount Ranier was especially dangerous because of the recent rock slides.* **Assent** can be a noun or a verb. As a verb **assent** means "to concur, to express agreement": *The union representative assented to the agreement.*

As a noun, **assent** means "an agreement": *The assent was not reached peacefully.*

assistance/assistants **Assistance** is a noun that means "help, support": *Please give us your assistance here for a moment.* **Assistants** is a plural noun that means "helpers": *Since the assistants were late, we found ourselves running behind schedule.*

assure, ensure, insure **Assure** is a verb that means "to promise": *The plumber assured us that the sink would not clog again.* **Ensure** and **insure** are both verbs that mean "to make certain," although some writers use **insure** solely for legal and financial writing and **ensure** for more widespread usage: *Since it is hard to insure yourself against mudslide, we did not buy the house on the hill. We left late to ensure that we would not get caught in traffic.*

at Avoid using **at** after "where": *Where are you seeing her (not "at")?*

at this point in time Although the term **at this point in time** is widely used (especially in politics), many consider it verbose and stuffy. Instead, use "now" or "at this time": *We are not now ready to discuss the new budget.*

awful/awfully Avoid using **awful** or **awfully** to mean "very" in formal discourse: *We* *had an awfully busy time at the amusement park.*

Although the use of **awful** to mean "terrible" (rather than "inspiring awe") has permeated all levels of writing and speech, consider using in its place a word that most closely matches your intended meaning: *We had a wretched (not "awful") time because the park was hot, noisy, and crowded.*

awhile/a while Awhile is an adverb and is always spelled as one word: *We visited awhile.* A while is a noun phrase (an article and a noun) and is used after a preposition: *We visited for a while.* The one-word form is gaining popularity after prepositions: *We visited for awhile.*

backward/backwards In formal discourse, **backward** is preferred: *This stroke is easier if you use a backward motion* (adjective). *Counting backward from 100 can be an effective way to induce sleep* (adverb).

bad/badly Bad, an adjective, is used to describe a noun or pronoun. **Badly,** an adverb, is used to describe a verb, adjective, or another adjective. Thus: *She felt bad because her broken leg throbbed badly.*

bare/bear Bare is an adjective or a verb. As an adjective, **bare** means "naked, unadorned'': *The wall looked bare without the picture.* As a verb, **bare** means "to reveal": *He bared his soul.* **Bear** is a noun or a verb. As a noun, **bear** refers to the animal: *The teddy bear was named after Theodore Roosevelt.* As a verb, **bear** means to carry: *He bears a heavy burden.*

because/due to the fact that/since Because or since are preferred over the wordy phrase **due to the fact that**: *He wrote the report longhand because (not "due to the fact") his computer was broken.*

before/prior to Prior to is used most often in a legal sense: *Prior to settling the claim, the Smiths spent a week calling the attorney general's office.* Use **before** in almost all other cases: *Before we go grocery shopping, we sort the coupons we have clipped from the newspaper.*

being as/being that Avoid both **being as** and **being that** in formal writing. Instead, use "since" or "because." For example: *Since (or "because") you asked, I'll be glad to help.*

beside/besides Although both words can function as prepositions, they have different shades of meaning: **beside** means "next to"; **besides** means "in addition to" or "except": *Besides, Richard would prefer not to sit beside* *the dog. There is no one here besides John and me.* **Besides** is also an adverb meaning "in addition": *Other people besides you feel the same way about the dog.*

better/had better The verb "had" is necessary in the phrase **had better** and should be retained: *She had better return the lawn mower today.*

between you and I Pronouns that function as objects of prepositions are traditionally used in the objective case: *Please keep this between you and me. I would appreciate it if you could keep this between her and them.*

bi- Many words that refer to periods of time by using the prefix **bi-** are potentially confusing. Ambiguity is avoided by using the prefix **semi-,** meaning "twice each" *(semiweekly; semimonthly; semiannual)* or by using the appropriate phrases *(twice a week; twice each month; every two months; every two years).*

bias/prejudice Generally, a distinction is made between **bias** and **prejudice.** Although both words imply "a preconceived opinion" or a "subjective point of view" in favor of something or against it, **prejudice** is generally used to express unfavorable feelings.

blonde/blond A **blonde** indicates a woman or girl with fair hair and skin. **Blond,** as aⁿ adjective, refers to either sex *(My three blond children. He is a cute blond boy),* but **blonde,** as an adjective, still applies to women: *The blonde actress and her companion made the front page of the tabloid.* Usage of **blonde** is not as common today as it once was.

borrow/lend **Borrow** means "to take with the intention of returning": *The book you borrow from the library today is due back in seven days.* **Lend** means "to give with the intention of getting back": *I will lend you the rake, but I need it back by Saturday.* The two terms are not interchangeable.

borrow off/borrow from **Borrow off,** considered slang, is not used in formal speech and writing; **borrow from** is the preferred expression.

bottom line This overworked term is frequently used as a synonym for "outcome" or "the final result": *The bottom line is that we have to reduce inventory to maintain profits.* Careful writers and speakers eschew it for less shopworn descriptions

brake/break The most common meaning of **brake** as a noun is a device for slowing a vehicle: *The car's new brakes held on the steep incline.* **Brake** can also mean "a thicket" or "a species of fern." **Break,** a verb, means "to crack or make useless": *Please be especially careful that you don't break that vase.*

breath/breathe Breath, a noun, is the air taken in during respiration: *Her breath looked like fog in the frosty morning air.* **Breathe,** a verb, refers to the process of inhaling and exhaling air: *"Please breathe deeply,"* the doctor said to the patient.

bring/take Bring is to carry toward the speaker: *She brings it to me.* **Take** is to carry away from the speaker: *She takes it away.*

bunch Use the noun **bunch** in formal writing only to refer to clusters of things grouped together, such as grapes or bananas: *That bunch of grapes looks better than the other one.* In formal writing, use *group* or *crowd* to refer to gatherings of people; **bunch** is used to refer to groups of people or items only in speech and informal writing.

burst, bursted/bust, busted Burst is a verb meaning "to come apart suddenly." The word **busted** is not acceptable in either speech or writing. Both **bust** and **busted** are slang; as such, they should not be used in formal writing, although they are acceptable in speech and informal writing.

but however/but yet There is no reason to combine **but** with another conjunction: *She* *said she was leaving, yet (not "but yet") she poured another cup of coffee.*

but that/but what As with the previous example, there is no reason to add the word **but** to either **that** or **what**: *We don't doubt that (not "but that") you will win this hand.*

but which/but who But should not be used before a clause starting with **which** or **who**: *It is a necessary improvement which (not "but which") will help matters greatly.*

buy/by Buy, a verb, means to "acquire goods at a price": *We have to buy a new dresser.* By can be a preposition, an adverb, or an adjective. As a preposition, **by** means "next to": *I pass by the office building every day.* As an adverb, **by** means "near, at hand": *The office is close by.* As an adjective, **by** means "situated to one side": *They came down on a by passage.*

calculate/figure/reckon None of these words is an acceptable substitute for *expect* or *imagine* in formal writing, although they are used in speech and informal prose.

can/may Traditionally, **may** is used in formal writing to convey permission; **can,** ability or capacity. In speech, however, the terms are used interchangeably to mean permission: *Can (May) I borrow your hedge clippers?* **Can** and **may** are frequently but not always interchangeable when used to mean possibility: *A blizzard can (or may) occur any time during February.* In negative constructions, **can't** is more common than **mayn't,** the latter being rare: *You can't eat that taco in the den.*

cannot/can not Cannot is occasionally spelled **can not.** The one-word spelling is by far the more common. The contradiction **can't** is used mainly in speech and informal writing.

can't help but Can't help but, as in *You can't help but like her,* is a double negative. This idiom can be replaced by the informal **can't help** or the formal **cannot but** where each is appropriate: *She can't help wishing that it was spring. I cannot but wish things had turned out differently.* While **can't help but** is common in all types of speech, avoid using it in formal writing.

canvas/canvass Canvas, a noun, refers to a heavy cloth: *The boat's sails are made of canvas.* Canvass, a verb, means "to solicit votes": *The candidate's representatives canvass the neighborhood seeking support.*

capital/Capitol Capital is the city or town that is the seat of government: *Paris is the* *capital of France*. **Capitol** refers to the building in Washington, D.C., in which the U.S. Congress meets: *When I was a child, we went for a visit to the Capitol building*. When used with a lowercase letter, **capitol** is the building of a state legislature. **Capital** also means "a sum of money": *After the sale of their home, they had a great deal of capital*. As an adjective, **capital** means "foremost" or "first-rate": *He was a capital fellow*.

cause of ... on account of/due to The phrases **on account of** and **due to** are unnecessary with **cause of.** Omit the phrases or revise the entire sentence: *One cause of physical and psychological problems is due to too much stress.* Change the sentence to: *Too much stress causes physical and psychological problems.*

censor/censure Although both words are verbs, they have different meanings. To **censor** is to remove something from public view on moral or other grounds, and to **censure** is to give a formal reprimand: *The committee censored the offending passages from the book and censured the librarian for placing it on the shelves.*

center around/center on Although both phrases are often criticized for being illogical, they have been used in writing for more than a hundred years to express the notion of collecting or gathering as if around a center point. The phrase *revolve around* is often suggested as an alternative, and the prepositions *at, in,* and *on* are considered acceptable with **center** in the following sense: *Their problems centered on their lack of expertise.*

chair/chairperson **Chairperson** is used widely in academic and governmental circles as an alternative to "chairman" or "chairwoman." While some cities reject the term **chairperson** as clumsy and unnecessary and use the term **chair** for any presiding officer, regardless of sex, **chairperson** is still standard in all types of writing and speech.

choose/chose **Choose** is a verb that means "to select one thing in preference to another": *Why choose tomatoes when they are out of season?* **Chose** is the past tense of "to choose": *I chose tomatoes over cucumbers at the salad bar.*

cite/sight/site To **cite** means to "quote a passage": *The scholar often cited passages from noted authorities to back up his opinions.* **Sight** is a noun that means "vision": *With her new glasses, her sight was once again perfect.* **Site** is a noun that means "place or location": *They picked out a beautiful site overlooking a lake for their new home.*

climatic/climactic The word **climatic** comes from the word "climate" and refers to weather: *This summer's brutal heat may indicate a climatic change.* **Climactic,** in contrast, comes from the word "climax" and refers to a point of high drama: *In the climactic last scene the hideous creature takes over the world.*

clothes/cloths **Clothes** are garments: *For his birthday, John got some handsome new clothes.* **Cloths** are pieces of fabric: *Use these cloths to clean the car.*

coarse/course **Coarse,** an adjective, means "rough or common": *The horsehair fabric was too coarse to be made into a pillow. Although he's a little coarse around the edges, he has a heart of gold.* **Course,** a noun, means "a path" or "a prescribed number of classes": *They followed the bicycle course through the woods. My courses include English, math, and science.*

complement/compliment Both words can function as both nouns and verbs. The noun **complement** means "that which completes or makes perfect": *The rich chocolate mousse was a perfect complement to the light meal.* The verb **complement** means "to complete": *The oak door complemented the new siding and windows.* The noun **compliment** means "an expression of praise or admiration": *The mayor* *paid the visiting officials the compliment of escorting them around town personally.* The verb **compliment** means "to pay a compliment to": *Everyone complimented her after the presentation.*

complementary/complimentary **Complementary** is an adjective that means "forming a complement, completing": *The complementary colors suited the mood of the room.* **Complimentary** is an adjective that means "expressing a compliment": *The complimentary reviews ensured the play a long run.* **Complimentary** also means "free": *We thanked them for the complimentary tickets.*

conformity to/conformity with Although the word **conformity** can be followed by either "to" or "with," **conformity to** is generally used when the idea of obedience is implied: *The new commissioner issued a demand for conformity to health regulation.* **Conformity with** is used to imply agreement or correspondence: *This is an idea in conformity with previous planning.*

consensus/consensus of The expression **consensus of** (*consensus of opinion*) is considered redundant, and the preferred usage is the single plural noun **consensus,** meaning "general agreement or concord": *Since the consensus was overwhelming, the city planners* *moved ahead with the proposal.* The phrase *general consensus* is also considered redundant. Increasingly, the word **consensus** is widely used attributively, as in the phrase *consensus politics.*

contact The word is both a verb and a noun. As a verb, it is frequently used imprecisely to mean "to communicate" when a more exact word (*telephone, write to, consult*) would better communicate the idea. **Contact** is a noun meaning "a person through whom one can obtain information" is now standard usage: *He is my contact in the state department.*

continual/continuous Use **continual** to mean "intermittent, repeated often" and **continuous** to mean "uninterrupted, without stopping": *We suffered intermittent losses of electricity during the hurricane. They had uninterrupted phone service during the hurricane.* **Continuous** and **continual** are never interchangeable with regard to spatial relationships: *One writer postulated that life is a continuous series of passages.*

corps/corpse Both words are nouns. A **corps** is a group of people acting together; the word is often used in a military context: *The officers' corps assembled before dawn for the drill.* A **corpse** is a dead body: *The corpse was in the morgue.*

counsel/council **Counsel** is a verb meaning "to give advice": *They counsel recovering gamblers.* **Council** is a noun meaning "a group of advisors": *The trade union council meets in Ward Hall every Thursday.*

couple/couple of Both phrases are informally used to mean "two" or "several": *I need a couple more cans of spackle. I took a couple of aspirins for my headache.* The expression **a couple of** is used in standard English, especially in referring to distance, money, or time: *He is a couple of feet away. I have a couple of thousand dollars in the bank. The store will open in a couple of weeks.* **Couple** may be treated as either singular or plural.

credible/creditable/credulous These three adjectives are often confused. **Credible** means "believable": *The tale is unusual, but seems credible to us.* **Creditable** means "worthy": *Sandra sang a creditable version of the song.* **Credulous** means "gullible": *The credulous Marsha believed that the movie was true.*

criteria/criterion **Criteria** is the plural of **criterion** (a standard for judgment). For example: *Of all their criteria for evaluating job performance, customer satisfaction was the most important criterion.*

data/datum **Data** is the plural of **datum** (fact). Although **data** is often used as a singular, it should still be treated as plural in formal speech and writing: *The data pertain (not "pertains") to the first half of the experiment.* To avoid awkward constructions, most writers prefer to use a more commonplace term such as "fact" or "figure" in place of **datum.**

descent/dissent Descent, a noun, means "downward movement": *Much to their surprise, their descent down the mountain was harder than their ascent had been.* **Dissent,** a verb, means "to disagree": *The town council strongly dissented with the proposed measure.* **Dissent** as a noun means "difference in sentiment or opinion": *Dissent over the new proposal caused a rift between colleagues.*

desert/dessert Desert as a verb means to abandon; as a noun, an arid region: *People deserted in the desert rarely survive.* **Dessert,** a noun, refers to the sweet served as the final course of a meal: *My sister's favorite dessert is strawberry shortcake.*

device/devise Device is a noun meaning "invention or contrivance": *Do you think that device will really save us time?* **Devise** is a verb meaning "to contrive or plan": *Did he devise some device for repairing the ancient pump assembly?*

die/dye Die, as a verb, means "to cease to live": *The frog will die if released from his*

aquarium into the pond. **Dye** as a verb means
''to color or stain something'': *I dye the drapes
to cover the stains.*

differ from/differ with **Differ from** means
''to be unlike''; **differ with** means ''to disagree with'': *The sisters differ from each other
in their attitudes. We differ with you on this
matter.*

different from/different than Although **different from** is the preferred usage (*His attitude is different from mine*), **different than** is
widely accepted when a clause follows, especially when the word ''from'' would create an
awkward sentence. Thus, *It's a different place
now than it was in the past* is preferable to *It's
a different place now from the place it used to
be.*

discreet/discrete **Discreet** means ''tact-
ful''; **discrete,** ''separate.'' For example: *Do
you have a discreet way of refusing the invita-
tion? The mosaic is made of hundreds of discrete pieces of tile.*

disinterested/uninterested **Disinterested**
is used to mean ''without prejudice, impar-
tial'' (*He is a disinterested judge*) and **uninterested** to mean ''bored'' or ''lacking
interest.'' (*They are completely uninterested in
sports*).

dominant/dominate Dominant, an adjective, means "ruling, controlling": *Social scientists have long argued over the dominant motives for human behavior.* **Dominate,** a verb, means "to control": *Advice columnists often preach that no one can dominate you unless you allow them to.*

don't/does not Don't is the contraction for "do not," not for **does not,** as in *I don't care, she doesn't (not don't) care.*

done Using **done** as an adjective to mean "through, finished" is standard. Originally, **done** was used attributively (*The pact between them was a done thing*), but it has become more common as a compliment: *Are your pictures done yet? When we were done with the power saw, we removed the blade.*

double negatives Although the use of double negatives (*They never paid no dues*) was standard for many years in English, today certain uses of the double negative are universally considered unacceptable: *He didn't have nothing to do,* for example. In educated speech and writing, "anything" would be used in place of "nothing."

doubt that/doubt whether/doubt if Doubt that is used to express conviction (*I doubt that they intended to hurt your feelings*); **doubt**

whether and **doubt if** are used to indicate uncertainty: *I doubt whether (or if) anyone really listened to the speaker.*

due to In formal discourse, **due to** is acceptable only after a form of the verb "to be": *Her aching back was due to poor posture.* **Due to** is not acceptable as a preposition meaning "because of" or "owing to": *Because of (not "due to") the poor weather, the bus was late.* Consider replacing **due to** with "because of" or "owing to."

each When **each** is used as a pronoun, it takes a singular verb (*Each was born in Europe*), although plurals are increasingly used in formal speech and writing in an attempt to avoid using "he" or "his" for sentences that include females or do not specify sex (*Each of them had their (rather than "his") own agenda.* More and more, the same pattern of pronoun agreement is being used with the singular pronouns *anyone, anybody, everyone, everybody, no one, someone,* and *somebody.* When the pronoun **each** is followed by an "of" phrase containing a plural noun or pronoun, usage guides suggest that the verb be singular, but the plural is used often even in formal writing: *Each of the children has (or "have") had a school physical.*

When the adjective **each** follows a plural subject, the verb agrees with the subject: *The rooms each have separate thermostats.*

each and every Use "each" or "every" in place of the phrase **each and every,** generally considered wordy: *Each of us enjoyed the concert. Every one of us stayed until the end of the performance.*

each other/one another Each other is traditionally used to indicate two members; **one another** for three or more: *The two children trade lunches with each other. The guests greeted one another fondly.* In standard practice, though, these distinctions are not observed in either speech or writing.

elicit/illicit Elicit, a verb, means "call forth"; **illicit,** an adjective, means "against the law": *The assault elicited a protest against illicit handguns.*

emigrate/immigrate Emigrate means "to leave one's own country to settle in another": *She emigrated from France.* **Immigrate** means "to enter a different country and settle there": *My father immigrated to America when he was nine years old.*

eminent/imminent Eminent means "distinguished": *Marie Curie was an eminent scientist in the final years of her life.* **Imminent** means "about to happen": *The thundershower seemed imminent.*

enthused/enthusiastic The word enthused

is used informally to mean "showing enthusiasm." For formal writing and speech, use the adjective **enthusiastic:** *The team was enthusiastic about the quarterback's winning play.*

envelop/envelope Envelop is a verb that means "to surround": *The music envelops him in a soothing atmosphere.* **Envelope,** a noun, is a flat paper container, usually for a letter: *Be sure to put a stamp on the envelope before you mail that letter.*

especially/specially The two words are not interchangeable: **especially** means "particularly"; **specially** means "for a specific reason." For example: *I especially value my wedding ring; it was made specially for me.*

-ess–or–er The suffix **-ess** has often been used to denote feminine nouns. While many such words are still in use, English is moving increasingly toward nouns that do not denote sex differences. The most widely observed guideline today is that if the sex of the performer is not relevant to the performance of the task or function, the neutral ending **-or** or **-er** should be used in place of **-ess.** Thus, words such as *ambassadress, ancestress, authoress, poetess, proprietress, sculptress* are no longer used; and the airlines, for example, have replaced both *steward* and *stewardess* with *flight attendant.*

et al. Et al., the Latin abbreviation for "and other people," is fully standard for use in a citation to refer to works with more than three authors: *Harris et al.*

Etc. Since **etc.** (et cetera) is the Latin abbreviation for "and other things," it should not be used to refer to people. In general, it should be avoided in formal writing as imprecise. In its place, provide the entire list of items.

-ette English nouns whose **-ette** ending signifies a feminine role or identity are passing out of usage. *Farmerette, suffragette, usherette,* for example, have been replaced by *farmer, suffragist,* and *usher,* respectively.

ever so often/every so often Ever so often means happening very often and **every so often** means happening occasionally.

everybody, every body/everyone, every one Everybody and everyone are indefinite pronouns: *Everybody likes William, and everyone enjoys his company.* Every body is a noun modified by "every" and and every one is a pronoun modified by "every"; both refer to a person in a specific group and are usually followed by "of": *Every body of water in our area is polluted; every one of our ponds is covered in debris.*

everyday/every day Everyday is an adjective that means "used daily, typical, ordinary"; **every day** is made up of a noun modified by the adjective "every" and means "each day": *Every day they had to deal with the everyday business of life.*

everywheres/everywhere Everywheres is a nonstandard term for **everywhere** and should be avoided in speech and writing.

exam/examination Exam should be reserved for everyday speech and **examination** for formal writing: *The College Board examinations are scheduled for this Saturday morning at 9:00.*

except for the fact that/except that Use **except that** in place of the verbose phrase **except for the fact that**: *Except that (not "except for the fact that") the button is missing, this is a lovely skirt.*

explicit/implicit Explicit means "stated plainly"; **implicit** means "understood," "implied": *You know we have an implicit understanding that you are not allowed to watch any television shows that contain explicit sex.*

fair/fare Fair as an adjective means "free from bias," "ample," "unblemished," "of light hue," or "attractive." As an adverb, it means "favorably." It is used informally to mean "honest." **Fare** as a noun means "the price charged for transporting a person" or "food."

farther/further Traditionally, **farther** is used to indicate physical distance (*Is it much farther to the hotel?*) and **further** is used to refer to additional time, amount, or abstract ideas (*Your mother does not want to talk about this any further*). This distinction, however, is rarely observed in everyday speech and writing.

fewer/less Traditionally, **fewer,** a plural noun, has most often been used to refer to individual units that can be counted: *There are fewer buttons on this shirt. No fewer than forty of the fifty voters supported the measure.* **Less,** a singular noun, is used to refer to uncountable quantities: *I have less patience that I used to.* Uncountable quantities are usually singular mass nouns (*Use less salt*) and singular abstract nouns (*There is less decency in the world today*).

Standard English does not usually reflect these distinctions, however. When followed by "than," **less** is used as often as **fewer** to indicate plural nouns that refer to items that can be counted: *There were no less than eight million people. No less than forty of the fifty voters supported the measure.*

figuratively/literally **Figuratively,** meaning "involving a figure of speech," usually implies that the statement is not true. **Literally,** meaning "actually, without exaggeration," implies that the statement is true: *The poet Robert Frost once figuratively described writing poetry without regular meter and rhyme as playing tennis with the net down. My sister literally passed out when she saw what had happened to her new car.*

   Literally is commonly used as an intensifier meaning "in effect, virtually": *The state representative was literally buried alive in the caucus.* This usage should be avoided in formal discourse.

fix The verb **fix,** meaning "to repair," is fully accepted in all areas of speech and writing. The noun **fix,** meaning "repair" or "adjustment," is used informally.

fixing to/intend to Use **intend to** in place of the colloquial term **fixing to:** *The community intends to (not "is fixing to") raise money to help the victims of the recent fire.*

flaunt/flout **Flaunt** means "to show off"; **flout,** "to ignore or treat with disdain." For example: *They flouted convention when they flaunted their wealth.*

flunk/fail Use the standard term **fail** in

speech and writing; **flunk** is a colloquial substitute.

former/latter **Former** is used to refer to the first of two items; **latter,** the second: *We enjoy both gardening and painting, the former during the summer and the latter during the winter.* When dealing with three or more items, use "first" and "last" rather than **former** and **latter:** *We enjoy gardening, painting, and skiing, but the last is very costly.*

formally/formerly Both words are adverbs. **Formally** means "in a formal manner": *The minister addressed the king and queen formally.* **Formerly** means "previously": *Formerly, he worked as a chauffeur; now, he is employed as a guard.*

forth/fourth **Forth** is an adverb meaning "going forward or away": *From that day forth, they lived happily ever after.* **Fourth** is most often used as an adjective that means "next after the third": *Mitchell was the fourth in line.*

fortuitous **Fortuitous** means "happening accidentally": *A fortuitous meeting with a former acquaintance led to a change in plans.* It is not a synonym for "lucky" or "fortunate."

from whence Although the phrase **from whence** is sometimes criticized on the grounds that "from" is redundant because it is included in the meaning of "whence," the idiom is nonetheless standard in both speech and writing: *She finally moved to Kansas, from whence she began to build a new life.*

fulsome Originally, **fulsome** meant "abundant," but for hundreds of years the word has been used to mean "offensive, disgusting, or excessively lavish." While the word still maintains the connotations of "excessive" or "offensive," it has also come to be used in the original sense as well: *Compare the severe furniture of the living room to the fulsome decorations in the den.*

fun **Fun** should not be used as an adjective in formal writing. Instead, substitute a word such as "happy," "pleasant," or "entertaining": *They had a pleasant (not "fun") afternoon at the park.*

gentleman Once used only to refer to men of high social rank, the term **gentleman** now also specifies a man of courtesy and consideration: *He behaves like a gentleman.* It is also used as a term of polite reference and address in the singular and plural: *This gentleman is waiting to be served. Are we ready to begin, gentlemen?*

get The verb **get** is used in many slang and colloquial phrases as a substitute for forms of "to be." For example: *They won't get accepted with that attitude.* In American English, an alternative past participle is **gotten,** especially in the sense of "received" and "acquired": *I have gotten (or "got") all I ever wanted.*

Both **have** and **has got** (meaning "must") are occasionally criticized as being redundant, but are nonetheless fully standard in all varieties of speech and writing: *You have got to carry your driver's licence at all times.*

good/well Good, an adjective, should be used to describe someone or something: *Joe is a good student.* **Well,** when used as an adverb, should describe an action: *She and Laura play well together on the swing set.* **Well,** when used as an adjective after "look," "feel" or other linking verbs, often refers to good health: *You're looking well.*

good and/very Avoid using **good and** as a substitute for **very:** *I was very (not "good and") hungry.*

graduate The passive form, once considered the only correct usage, is seldom used today: *I was graduated from the Merchant Marine Academy last May.* Although some critics condemn the use of **graduate** as a transitive verb meaning "to receive a degree or diploma from," its use is increasing in both speech and writing: *She graduated from elementary school in Cleveland.*

great The word **great** has been overused in informal writing and speech as a synonym for "enthusiastic," "good," or "clever": *She was really great at making people feel at home.*

had drank/had drunk Some authorities accept **had drank** as acceptable usage: *I had drank a gallon of milk.* **Had drunk,** though, is fully standard and the preferred usage.

has/have; has got/have got The word "got" is unnecessary; simply use **has** or **have:** *Jessica has a mild case of chicken pox.*

had ought/ought Had ought is considered wordy; the preferred usage is **ought:** *She ought (not "had ought") to heed her mother's advice.*

half/a half a/a half Use either **half** or **a half;** a half a is considered wordy: *Please give me a half (not "a half a") piece. I'd like half that slice, please.*

hanged/hung Although both words are past-tense forms of "to hang," **hanged** is used to refer to executions (*Billy Budd was hanged*) and **hung** is used for all other meanings: *The stockings were hung by the chimney with care.*

have/of Use **have** rather than **of** after helping verbs like "could," "should," "would," "may," and "might": *They should have (not "of") let me know of their decision earlier.*

healthy/healthful **Healthy** means "possessing health"; **healthful** means "bringing about health": *They believed that they were healthy people because they ate healthful food.*

he, she; he/she The pronouns **he** and **she** refer to male and female antecedents, respectively. Traditionally, when an antecedent in singular form could be either female or male, "he" was always used to refer to either sex: *A child is often apprehensive when he first begins school.* Today, however, various approaches have been developed to avoid the all-purpose "he." Many people find the construction *he/she* awkward: *A child is often apprehensive when he/she first begins school.* The blended form *s/he* has not been widely adopted, probably because of confusion over pronunciation. Most people now favor either rephrasing the sentence entirely to omit the pronoun or reconstructing the sentence in the third-person plural: *Children are often apprehensive when they first begin school.*

hopefully **Hopefully** means "with hope": *They waited hopefully for a look at the astronaut.* In formal writing and speech, avoid us-

ing **hopefully** to mean "it is to be hoped":
*We hope (not "Hopefully") Captain Smith will
come out of the hangar soon.*

how come/why How come is used informally in speech to substitute for **why.**

human/humane Both words are adjectives.
Human means "pertaining to humanity": *The
subject of the documentary is the human race.*
Humane means "tender, compassionate, or
sympathetic": *Many of her patients believed
that her humane care speeded their recovery.*

idea/ideal Idea means "thought," while
ideal means "a model of perfection" or
"goal." The two words are not interchangeable. They should be used as follows: *The idea
behind the blood drive is that our ideals often
move us to help others.*

if/whether Use **whether** rather than **if** to
begin a subordinate clause when the clause
states a choice: *I don't know whether (not
"if") I should stay until the end or leave right
after the opening ceremony.*

impact Both the noun and verb **impact** are
used to indicate forceful contact: *I cannot
overstate the impact of the new policy on productivity.* Avoid using **impact** as a verb to

mean "to have an effect," as in *Our work here impacts on every division in the firm.*

imply/infer Imply means "to suggest without stating": *The message on Karen's postcard implies that her vacation has not turned out as she wished.* **Infer** means "to reach a conclusion based on understood evidence": *From her message I infer that she wishes she had stayed home.* When used in this manner, the two words describe two sides of the same process.

in/into In is used to indicate condition or location, "positioned within": *She was in labor. The raccoon was in the wood pile.* **Into,** in contrast, indicates movement or a change in condition "from the outside to the inside": *The raccoon went into the shed. He went into cardiac arrest.* **Into** is also used as a slang expression for "involved with" or "interested in": *They are really into health foods.*

in Several phrases beginning with in are verbose and should be avoided in formal writing. Refer to the following chart:

Replace the phrase . . .
in this day and age

With . . .
now

Replace the phrase . . .
in spite of the fact that

With . . .
although *or* even though

Replace the phrase . . .
in the neighborhood of

With . . .
approximately *or* about

Replace the phrase . . .
in the event that

With . . .
if

The following phrases can be omitted entirely: *in a very real sense, in number, in nature, in reality, in terms of,* and *in the case of.*

inferior than Inferior to and **worse than** are the generally preferred forms: *This wine is inferior to (not "inferior than") the burgundy we had last night.*

incredible/incredulous Incredible means "cannot be believed"; **incredulous** means "unbelieving": *The teacher was incredulous when she heard the pupil's incredible story about the fate of his term project.*

individual/person/party **Individual** should be used to stress uniqueness or to refer to a single human being as contrasted to a group of people: *The rights of the individual should not supersede the rights of a group.* **Person** is the preferred word in other contexts: *What person wouldn't want to have a chance to sail around the world?* **Party** is used to refer to a group: *Send the party of five this way, please.* **Party** is also used to refer to an individual mentioned in a legal document.

ingenious/ingenuous **Ingenious** means "resourceful, clever": *My sister is ingenious when it comes to turning leftovers into something delicious.* **Ingenuous** means "frank, artless": *The child's ingenuous manner is surprising considering her fame.*

in regards to/with regards to Both terms are considered nonstandard terms for "in regard to," "with regard to," and "as regards." *As regards (not "in regards to") your request of April 1, we have traced your shipment and it will be delivered tomorrow.*

inside/outside; inside of/outside of When the words **inside** and **outside** are used as prepositions, the word **of** is not included: *Stay inside the house. The authorization is outside my department.* **Inside of** is used informally to refer to time (*I'll be there inside of an hour*), but in formal speech or writing **within** is the preferred usage: *The dump was cleaned up within a month.*

insignia Insignia was originally the plural of the Latin word "insigne." The plural term **insignias** has been standard usage since the eighteenth century.

irregardless/regardless Regardless is the standard term; avoid **irregardless** in both speech and writing.

is when/is where Both phases are unacceptable and are to be avoided.

its/it's/its' Its is the possessive form if *it: The shrub is losing its blossoms.* **It's** is the contraction for *it is: It's a nice day.* The two are often confused because possessives are most frequently formed with *-'s.* **Its'** is nonstandard usage.

It's me/It's I The traditional rule is that personal pronouns after the verb "to be" take the nominative case (*I, she, he, we, they*). Today, however, such usage as *it's me, that's him, it must be them* are almost universal in informal speech. The objective forms have also replaced the nominative forms in informal speech in such constructions as *me neither, who, them?* In formal discourse, however, the nominative forms are still used: *it's I, that's he.*

-ize/-wise Use the suffix **-ize** to change a noun or adjective into a verb: *categorize*. Use the suffix **-wise** to change a noun or adjective into an adverb: *otherwise*.

kind of/sort of/type of Avoid using either **kind of, sort of,** or **type of** as synonyms for "somewhat" in formal speech and writing. Instead, use **rather**: *She was rather (not "kind of") slender.* It is acceptable to use the three terms only when the word **kind, sort,** or **type** is stressed: *This kind of cheese is hard to digest.* Do not add "a": *I don't know what kind of (not "kind of a") cheese that is.* When the word **kind, sort,** or **type** is not stressed, omit the phrase entirely: *That's an unusual (not "unusual kind of") car. She's a pleasant (not "pleasant sort of a") person.*

later/latter **Later** is used to refer to time; **latter,** the second of two items named: *It is later than you think. Of the two shirts I just purchased, I prefer the latter.* See also **former/ latter.**

lay/lie **Lay** is a transitive verb that means "to put down" or "to place." It takes a direct object: *Please lay the soup spoon next to the teaspoon.* **Lie** is an intransitive verb that means "to be in a horizontal position" or "be situated." It does not take a direct object: *The puppy lies down where the old dog had always lain. The hotel lies on the outskirts of town.* The confusion arises over **lay,** which is the present tense of the verb **lay** and the past tense of the verb **lie.**

To lie (recline)

Present: Spot lies (is lying) down.
Future: Spot will lie down.
Past: Spot lay down.
Perfect: Spot has (had, will have) lain down.

To lay (put down)

Present: He lays (is laying) his dice down.
Future: He will lay his dice down.
Past: He laid his dice down.
Perfect: He has (had, will have) laid his dice down.

Although **lie** and **lay** tend to be used interchangeably in all but the most careful, formal speech, the following phrases are generally considered nonstandard and are avoided in written English: *Lay down, dears. The dog laid in the sun. Abandoned cars were laying in the junkyard. The reports have laid in the mailbox for a week.*

lead/led Lead as a verb means "to take or conduct on the way": *I plan to lead a quiet* *afternoon.* **Led** is the past tense: *He led his followers through the dangerous underbrush.* **Lead,** as a noun, means "a type of metal": *Pipes are made of lead.*

learn/teach **Learn** is to acquire knowledge: *He learned fast.* **Teach** is to impart knowledge: *She taught well.*

leave/let **Leave** and **let** are interchangeable only when followed by the word "alone": *Leave him alone. Let him alone.* In other instances, **leave** means "to depart" or "permit to remain in the same place": *If you leave, please turn off the copier. Leave the extra paper on the shelf.* **Let** means "to allow": *Let him work with the assistant, if he wants.*

lessen/lesson **Lessen** is a verb meaning "to decrease": *To lessen the pain of a burn, apply ice to the injured area.* **Lesson** is most often used as a noun meaning "material assigned for study": *Today, the lesson will be on electricity.*

let's **Let's** is often used as a word in its own right rather than as the contraction of "let us." As such, it is often used in informal speech and writing with redundant or appositional pronouns: *Let's us take in a movie. Let's you and me go for a walk.* Usage guides suggest avoiding **let's us** in formal speech and writing, although both *let's you and me* and *let's* *you and I* occur in the everyday speech of educated speakers. While the former conforms to the traditional rules of grammar, the latter, nevertheless, occurs more frequently.

lightening/lightning **Lightening** is a form of the verb that means "to brighten": *The cheerful new drapes and bunches of flowers went a long way in lightening the room's somber mood.* **Lightning** is most often used as a noun to mean "flashes of light generated during a storm": *The thunder and lightning frightened the child.*

like/such as Use **like** to compare an example to the thing mentioned and **such as** to show that the example is representative of the thing mentioned: *Judy wants to be a famous clothing designer like John Weitz, Liz Claiborne, and Yves St. Laurent. Judy has samples of many fine articles such as evening dresses, suits, and jackets.*

Many writers favor not separating **such** and **as** with an intervening word: *samples of many fine articles such as* rather than *samples of such fine articles as.*

loose/lose **Loose** is an adjective meaning "free and unattached": *The dog was loose again.* **Loose** can also be a verb meaning "let loose": *The hunters loose the dogs as soon as the ducks fall.* **Lose** is a verb meaning "to part with unintentionally'': *He will lose his keys if he leaves them on the countertop.*

lots/lots of Both terms are used in informal speech and writing as a substitute for ''a great many,'' ''very many,'' or ''much.''

mad/angry Traditionally, **mad** has been used to mean ''insane''; **angry**, ''full of ire.'' While **mad** can be used to mean ''enraged, angry,'' in informal usage, you should replace **mad** with **angry** in formal discourse: *The president is angry at Congress for overriding his veto.*

male/masculine The term **male** is used to describe men and boys or attributes and conduct traditionally applied to them. **Male** can also be used to describe physical or sexual characteristics that can apply to a human, an animal, or a plant: *He is a male in his prime. There are two males and four females in the pride. These are the male parts of the flower.* **Masculine** refers to the traits a culture or society considers appropriate to or ideally associated with men and boys. In American and Western Europe culture these traits have traditionally included strength, aggressiveness, and courage: *He has a firm, masculine handshake.*

man **Man** refers both to adult male human beings as well as the possession of the typical or desirable masculine qualities: *He takes his punishment like a man.*

The use of the term **man** as a synonym for "human being," both by itself and in compounds (*mankind*), is declining. Terms such as *human being(s), human race, humankind, humanity, people,* and, when necessary, *men and women* or *women and men* are widely accepted in formal usage.

-man/-person The use of the term **man** as the last element in compound words referring to a person of either sex who performs some function (*anchorman, chairman, spokesman*) has declined in recent years. Now, such compound words are only widely used if the word refers to a male. The sex-neutral word **person** is otherwise substituted for **man** (*anchorperson, chairperson, spokesperson*). In other instances, a form without a suffix (*anchor, chair*), or a word that does not denote gender (*speaker*) is used.

The compound words *freshman, lowerclassmen, underclassmen* are still generally used in schools and Congress as well, and are applied to members of both sexes. As a modifier, *freshman* is used with both singular and plural nouns: *freshman athlete, freshman legislators.* See also **chair/chairperson.**

manly/manful/mannish While all three words mean "having traits or qualities characteristics of or appropriate to adult males,'' they carry different connotations. Both **manly** and **manful** are terms of approval, suggesting such admirable traits as courage and strength: *He made a manful effort to overcome adversity.* **Mannish,** in contrast, is most often used derogatorily in referring to qualities of a woman that are more appropriate to a man: *There is a mannish abruptness in her speech. She wore a severely mannish hat.*

maybe/may be **Maybe,** an adverb, means ''perhaps'': *Maybe the newspapers can be recycled with the plastic and glass.* **May be,** a verb, means ''could be'' *It may be too difficult, however.*

me and **Me and** is considered nonstandard usage when part of a compound subject: *Bob and I (not ''Me and Bob'') decided to fly to Boston.*

media **Media,** the plural of **medium,** is used with a plural verb: *Increasingly, many of the radio and television media seem to be stressing sensational news.*

mighty **Mighty** is used informally for ''very'' or ''extremely'': *He is a mighty big fighter.*

moral/morale As a noun, **moral** means ''ethical lesson'': *Each of Aesop's fables has a* *clear moral.* **Morale** means "state of mind" or "spirit": *Her morale was lifted by her colleague's good wishes.*

more important/more importantly Both phrases are acceptable in standard English: *My donations of clothing were tax deductible; more important(ly), the clothes were given to homeless people.*

Ms. (or Ms) The title **Ms.** is widely used in business and professional circles as an alternative to "Mrs." and "Miss," both of which reveal a woman's marital status. Some women prefer "**Mrs.**," where appropriate, or the traditional "**Miss**," which is still fully standard for an unmarried woman or a woman whose marital status is unknown. Since **Ms.** is not an abbreviation, some sources spell it without a period; others use a period to parallel "Mr." It is correctly used before a woman's name but not before her husband's name: *Ms. Leslie Taubman* or *Ms. Taubman* (not *"Ms. Steven Taubman"*).

much/many Use **many** rather than **much** to modify plural nouns: *They had many (not "much") dogs. There were too many (not "much") facts to absorb.*

Muslim/Moslem **Muslim** is now the preferred form for an adherent of Islam, though **Moslem,** the traditional form, is still in use.

mutual One current meaning of **mutual** is "reciprocal": *Employers and employees sometimes suffer from a mutual misunderstanding.* **Mutual** can also mean "held in common; shared": *Their mutual goal is clearly understood.*

myself; herself; himself; yourself The -self pronouns are intensive or reflexive, intensifying or referring to an antecedent: *Kerri herself said so. Mike and I did it ourselves.* Questions are raised when the -self forms are used instead of personal pronouns (I, me, etc.) as subjects, objects, or complements. This use of the -self forms is especially common in informal speech and writing: *Many came to welcome my wife and myself back from China.* All these forms are also used, alone or with other nouns or pronouns, after "as," "than," or "but" in all varieties of speech and writing: *Letters have arrived for everyone but the counselors and yourselves.* Although there is ample precedent in both British and American usage for the expanded uses of the -self constructions, the -self pronouns should be used in formal speech and writing only with the nouns and pronouns to which they refer: *No one except me (not "myself") saw the movie.*

nauseous/nauseated Nauseated is generally preferred in formal writing over **nauseous**: *The wild ride on the roller coaster made Wanda feel nauseated.*

neither . . . nor When used as a correlative, **neither** is almost always followed by **nor**: *neither Caitlyn nor her father . . .* The subjects connected by **neither . . . nor** take a singular verb when both subjects are singular (*Neither Caitlyn nor her father is going to watch the program*) and a plural verb when both are plural (*Neither the rabbits nor the sheep have been fed yet today*). When a singular and a plural subject are joined by these correlatives, the verb should agree with the nearer noun or pronoun: *Neither the mayor nor the council members have yielded. Neither the council members nor the mayor has yielded.*

nohow The word **nohow,** nonstandard usage for "in no way" or "in any way," should be avoided in speech and writing.

none None can be treated as either singular or plural depending on its meaning in a sentence. When the sense is "not any persons or things," the plural is more common: *The rescue party searched for survivors, but none were found.* When **none** is clearly intended to mean "not one" or "not any," it is followed by a singular verb: *Of all the ailments I have diagnosed during my career, none has been stranger than yours.*

no . . . nor/no . . . or Use **no . . . or** in compound phrases: *We had no milk or eggs in the house.*

nothing like, nowhere near Both phrases are used in informal speech and writing, but they should be avoided in formal discourse. Instead, use "**not nearly**": *The congealed pudding found in the back of the refrigerator is not nearly as old as the stale bread on the second shelf.*

nowheres/nowhere The word **nowheres,** nonstandard usage for **nowhere,** should be avoided in speech and writing.

of Avoid using **of** with descriptive adjectives after the adverbs "how" or "too" in formal speech and writing. This usage is largely restricted to informal discourse: *How long of a ride will it be? It's too cold of a day for swimming.*

off of/off **Off of** is redundant and awkward; use **off**: *The cat jumped off the sofa.*

OK/O.K./okay All three spellings are considered acceptable, but the phrases are generally reserved for informal speech and writing.

on account of/because of Since it is less wordy, **because of** is the preferred phrase: *Because of her headache, they decided to go straight home.*

on the one hand/on the other hand These two transitions should be used together: *On* *the one hand, we hoped for fair weather. On the other hand, we knew the rain was needed for the crops.* This usage, though, can be wordy. Effective substitutes include "in contrast," "but," "however," and "yet": *We hoped for fair weather, yet we knew the rain was needed for the crops.*

only The placement of **only** as a modifier is more a matter of style and clarity than of grammatical rule. In strict, formal usage, **only** should be placed as close as possible *before* the word it modifies. In the following sentence, for example, the placement of the word **only** suggests that no one but the children was examined: *The doctor examined only the children.* In the next sentence, the placement of **only** says that no one but the doctor did the examining: *Only the doctor examined the children.* Nonetheless, in all types of speech and writing, people often place **only** before the verb regardless of what it modifies. In spoken discourse, speakers may convey their intended meaning by stressing the word or construction to which **only** applies.

owing to the fact that "Because" is generally accepted as a less wordy substitute for **owing to the fact that**.

pair/pairs When modified by a number, the plural of **pair** is commonly **pairs**, especially when referring to persons: *The three pairs of costumed children led off Halloween parade.* The plural **pair** is used mainly in reference to inanimate objects or nonhumans: *There are four pair (or "pairs") of shoelaces. We have two pair (or "pairs") of rabbits.*

passed/past Passed is a form of the verb meaning "to go by": *Bernie passed the same buildings on his way to work each day.* **Past** can function as a noun, adjective, adverb, or preposition. As a noun, **past** means "the history of a nation, person, etc.": *The lessons of the past should not be forgotten.* As an adjective, **past** means "gone by or elapsed in time": *John is worried about his past deeds.* As an adverb, **past** means "so as to pass by": *The fire engine raced past the parked cars.* As a preposition, **past** means "beyond in time": *It's past noon already.*

patience/patients Patience, a noun, means "endurance": *Chrissy's patience makes her an ideal babysitter.* **Patients** are people under medical treatment: *The patients must remain in the hospital for another week.*

peace/piece Peace is "freedom from discord": *The negotiators hoped that the new treaty would bring about lasting peace.* **Piece** is "a portion of a whole" or "a short musical arrangement": *I would like just a small piece of* *cake, please. The piece in E flat is especially beautiful.*

people/persons In formal usage, **people** is most often included to refer to a general group, emphasizing anonymity: *We the people of the United States . . .* Use **persons** to indicate any unnamed individuals within the group: *Will the persons who left their folders on the table please pick them up at their earliest convenience.* Except when individuals are being emphasized, **people** is generally suggested for use rather than **persons**.

per; a/an **Per,** meaning ''for each,'' occurs mainly in technical or statistical contexts: *This new engine averages fifty miles per hour. Americans eat fifty pounds of chicken per person per year.* It is also frequently used in sports commentary: *He scored an average of two runs per inning.* **A** or **an** is often considered more suitable in nontechnical use: *The silk costs ten dollars a yard. How many miles an hour can you walk?*

percent/per cent **Percent** comes from the English *per cent.,* an abbreviation of the Latin *per centum.* It almost always follows a number: *I made 12 percent interest by investing my money in that new account.* In formal writing, use the word rather than the symbol (%). The use of the two-word form **per cent** is diminishing.

percent/percentage Percent is used with a number, **percentage** with a modifier. **Percentage** is used most often after an adjective: *A high percentage of your earnings this year is tax deductible.*

personal/personnel Personal means "private": *The lock on her journal showed that it was clearly personal.* **Personnel** refers to employees: *Attention all personnel!* The use of **personnel** as a plural has become standard in business and government: *The personnel were dispatched to the Chicago office.*

phenomena Like words such as **criteria** and **media, phenomena** is a plural form (of "**phenomenon**"), meaning "an observable fact, occurrence, or circumstance": *The official explained that the disturbing phenomena we had seen for the past three evenings were nothing more than routine aircraft maneuvers.*

plain/plane Plain as an adjective means "easily understood," "undistinguished," or "unadorned": *His meaning was plain to all. The plain dress suited the gravity of the occasion.* As an adverb, **plain** means "clearly and simply": *She's just plain foolish.* As a noun, **plain** is a flat area of land: *The vast plain seemed to go on forever.* As a noun, **plane** has a number of different meanings. It most commonly refers to an airplane, but is also used in mathematics and fine arts. As a verb, **plane** is a tool used to shave wood: *The carpenter used a plane to shave a half inch off the bottom of the door so it would clear the carpet.*

plenty As a noun, **plenty** is acceptable in standard usage: *I have plenty of money.* In informal speech and writing **plenty** is often a substitute for "**very**": *She was traveling plenty fast down the freeway.*

plus Plus is a preposition meaning "in addition to": *My salary plus overtime is enough to allow us a gracious lifestyle.* Recently, **plus** has been used as a conjunctive adverb in informal speech and writing: *My salary is larger than his; plus, I work fewer hours.* This usage is still considered nonstandard.

practicable/practical Practicable means "capable of being done": *My decorating plans were too difficult to be practicable.* **Practical** means "pertaining to practice or action": *It was just not practical to paint the floor white.*

practically Use **practically** as a synonym for "in effect," or "virtually." It is also considered correct to use it in place of "**nearly**" in all varieties of speech and writing.

precede/proceed Although both words are verbs, they have different meanings. **Precede**

means "to go before": *Morning precedes afternoon*. **Proceed** means "to move forward": *Proceed to the exit in an orderly fashion*.

presence/presents Presence is used chiefly to mean "attendance; close proximity": *Your presence at the ceremony will be greatly appreciated*. **Presents** are gifts: *Thank you for giving us such generous presents*.

previous to/prior to Before is generally preferred in place of either expression: *Before (not "previous to"/"prior to") repairing the tire, you should check to see if there are any other leaks*.

principal/principle Principal can be a noun or an adjective. As a noun, **principal** mean "chief or head official" (*The principal decided to close school early on Tuesday*) or "sum of capital" (*Invest only the interest, never the principal*). As an adjective, **principal** means "first or highest": *The principal ingredient is sugar*. **Principle** is a noun only, meaning "rule" or "general truth": *Regardless of what others said, she stood by her principles*.

providing/provided Both forms can serve as subordinating conjunctions meaning "on the condition that": *Provided (Providing) that we get the contract in time, we will be able to begin work by the first of the month*. While some critics feel that **provided** is more acceptable in formal discourse, both are correct.

question of whether/question as to whether Both phrases are wordy substitutes for "whether": *Whether (not "the question of whether"/"the question as to whether") it rains or not, we are planning to go on the hike.*

quiet/quite **Quiet,** as an adjective, means "free from noise": *When the master of ceremonies spoke, the room became quiet.* **Quite,** an adverb, means "completely, wholly": *By the late afternoon, the children were quite exhausted.*

quotation/quote **Quotation,** a noun, means "a passage quoted from a speech or book": *The speaker read a quotation of twenty-five lines to the audience.* **Quote,** a verb, means "to repeat a passage from a speech, etc.": *Marci often quotes from popular novels.* **Quote** and **quotation** are often used interchangeably in speech; in formal writing, however, a distinction is still observed between the two words.

rain/reign/rein As a noun, **rain** means "water that falls from the atmosphere to earth." As a verb, **rain** means "to send down; to give abundantly": *The crushed piñata rained candy on the eager children.* As a noun, **reign** means "royal rule": as a verb, "to have supreme control'': *The monarch's reign was marked by social unrest.* As a noun, **rein** means ''a leather strap used to guide an animal;'' as a verb, ''to control or guide'': *He used the rein to control the frisky colt.*

raise/rise/raze **Raise,** as a transitive verb that takes a direct object, means ''to elevate'': *How can I raise the cost of my house?* **Rise,** as an intransitive verb that does not take a direct object, means ''to go up, to get up'': *Will housing costs rise this year?* **Raze** is a transitive verb meaning ''to tear down, demolish'': *The wrecking crew was ready to raze the condemned building.*

rarely ever/rarely/hardly The term **rarely ever** is used informally in speech and writing. For formal discourse, use either **rarely** or **hardly** in place of **rarely ever:** *She rarely calls her mother. She hardly calls her mother.*

real/really In formal usage, **real** (an adjective meaning ''genuine'') should not be used in place of **really** (an adverb meaning ''actually''): *The platypus hardly looked real. How did it really happen?*

reason is because/reason is since Although both expression are commonly used in informal speech and writing, formal usage requires a clause beginning with ''that'' after "reason is": *The reason that the pool is empty is that (not "because" or "since") the town recently imposed a water restriction.* Another alternative is to recast the sentence: *The pool is empty because the town recently imposed a water restriction.*

regarding/in regard to/with regard to/relating to/relative to/with respect to/respecting All the above expressions are wordy substitutes for "about," "concerning," or "on": *Janet spoke about (not "relative to," etc.) the PTA's plans for the September fund drive.*

relate to The phrase **relate to** is used informally to mean "understand" or "respond in a favorable manner": *I don't relate to chemistry.* It is rarely used in formal writing or speech.

repeat it/repeat it again Repeat it is the expression to use to indicate someone should say something for a second time: *I did not hear your name; please repeat it.* **Repeat it again** indicates the answer is to be said a third time. In the majority of instances, **repeat it** is the desired phrase; **again** an unnecessary addition.

respectful/respective Respectful means "showing (or full of) respect": *If you are re-*

spectful toward others, they will treat you with consideration as well. **Respective** means "in the order given": *The respective remarks were made by executive board members Joshua Whittles, Kevin McCarthy, and Warren Richmond.*

reverend/reverent As an adjective (usually capitalized), **Reverend** is an epithet of respect given to a clergyman: *The Reverend Mr. Jones gave the sermon.* As a noun, a **reverend** is "a clergyman": *In our church, the reverend opens the service with a prayer.* **Reverent** is an adjective meaning "showing deep respect": *The speaker began his remarks with a reverent greeting.*

right/rite/write **Right** is used as an adjective to mean "proper, correct" and "as opposed to left"; as a noun to mean "claims or titles"; as an adverb to mean "in a straight line, directly"; as a verb to mean "to restore to an upright position." **Rite** is a noun meaning "a solemn ritual": *The religious leader performed the necessary rites.* **Write** is a verb meaning "to form characters on a surface": *The child liked to write her name over and over.*

says/said Use **said** rather than **says** after a verb in the past tense: *At the public meeting, he stood up and said (not "says"), "The bond issue cannot pass."*

seldom ever/seldom Seldom is the preferred form in formal discourse: *They seldom (not "seldom ever") visit the beach.*

sensual/sensuous Sensual carries sexual overtones: *The massage was a sensual experience.* Sensuous means "pertaining to the senses": *The sensuous aroma of freshly baked bread wafted through the house.*

set/sit Set, a transitive verb, describes something a person does to an object: *She set the book down on the table.* Sit, an intransitive verb, describes a person resting: *Marvin sits on the straight-backed chair.*

shall/will Today, shall is used for first-person questions requesting consent or opinion: *Shall we go for a drive? Shall I buy this dress or that?* Shall can also be used in the first person to create an elevated tone: *We shall call on you at six o'clock.* It is sometimes used with the second or third person to state a speaker's resolution: *You shall obey me.*

Traditionally, will was used for the second and third persons: *Will you attend the party? Will he and she go as well?* It is now widely used in speech and writing as the future-tense helping verb for all three persons: *I will drive, you will drive, they will drive.*

should/would Rules similar to those for choosing between "shall" and "will" have long been advanced for **should** and **would**. In current American usage, use of **would** far outweighs that of **should**. **Should** is chiefly used to state obligation: *I should repair the faucet. You should get the parts we need.* **Would,** in contrast, is used to express a hypothetical situation or a wish: *I would like to go. Would you?*

since **Since** is an adverb meaning "from then until now": *She was appointed in May and has been supervisor ever since.* It is also used as an adverb meaning "between a particular past time and the present, subsequently": *They had at first refused to cooperate, but have since agreed to volunteer.* As a preposition, **since** means "continuously from": *It has been rainy since June.* It is also used as a preposition meaning "between a past time or event and the present": *There have been many changes since the merger.* As a conjunction, **since** means "in the period following the time when": *He has called since he changed jobs.* **Since** is also used as a synonym for "because": *Since you're here early, let's begin.*

situation The word **situation** is often added unnecessarily to a sentence: *The situation is that we must get the painting done by the weekend.* In such instances, consider revising the sentence to pare excess words: *We must get the painting done by the weekend.*

slow/slowly Today **slow** is used chiefly in spoken imperative constructions with short verbs that express motion, such as "drive," walk, "swim," and "run." For example: *Drive slow, Don't walk so slow.* **Slow** is also combined with present participles to form adjectives: *He was slow-moving. It was a slow-burning fire.* **Slowly** is found commonly in formal writing and is used in both speech and writing before a verb (*He slowly walked through the hills*) as well as after a verb (*He walked slowly through the hills*).

so Many writers object to **so** being used as an intensifier, noting that in such usage it is often vague: *They were so happy.* **So** followed by "that" and a clause usually eliminates the vagueness: *They were so happy that they had been invited to the exclusive party.*

so/so that **So that,** rather than **so,** is most often used in formal writing to avoid the possibility of ambiguity: *He visited Aunt Lucia so that he could help her clear the basement.*

some **Some** is often used in informal speech and writing as an adjective meaning "exceptional, unusual" and as an adverb meaning "somewhat." In more formal instances, use "somewhat" in place of **some** as an adverb or a more precise word such as "remarkable" in place of **some** an adjective: *Those are unusual (not "some") shoes. My sister and brother-in-law are going to have to rush somewhat (not "some") to get here in time for dinner.*

somebody/some body Somebody is an indefinite pronoun: *Somebody recommended this restaurant.* **Some body** is a noun modified by an adjective: *I have a new spray that will give my limp hair some body.*

someone/some one Someone is an indefinite pronoun: *Someone who ate here said the pasta was delicious.* **Some one** is a pronoun adjective modified by "some": *Please pick some one magazine that you would like to read.*

someplace/somewhere Someplace should be used only in informal writing and speech; use **somewhere** for formal discourse.

sometime/sometimes/some time Traditionally, these three words have carried different meanings. **Sometime** means "at an unspecified time in the future": *Why not plan to visit Niagara Falls sometime?* **Sometimes** means "occasionally": *I visit my former college roommate sometimes.* **Some time** means "a span of time'': *I need some time to make up my mind about what you have said.*

somewheres Somewheres is not accepted in formal writing or speech; use the standard "somewhere": *She would like to go some-where (not "somewheres") special to celebrate New Year's Eve.*

split infinitive There is a long-standing convention that prohibits placing a word between "to" and the verb: *To understand fully another culture, you have to live among its people for many years.* This convention is based on an analogy with Latin, in which an infinitive is only one word and therefore cannot be divided. Criticism of the split infinitive was especially strong when the modeling of English on Latin was especially popular, as it was in the nineteenth century. Today many note that a split infinitive sometimes creates a less awkward sentence: *Many American companies expect to more than double their overseas investments in the next decade.*

stationary/stationery Although these two words sound alike, they have very different meanings. *Stationary* means "staying in one place": *From this distance, the satellite appeared to be stationary.* **Stationery** means "writing paper": *A hotel often provides stationery with its name preprinted.*

straight/strait Straight is most often used as an adjective meaning "unbending": *The path cut straight through the woods.* **Strait,** a noun, is "a narrow passage of water connecting two large bodies of water" or "distress, dilemma": *He was in dire financial straits.*

subsequently/consequently Subsequently means "occurring later, afterward": *We went to a new French restaurant for dinner; subsequently, we heard that everyone who had eaten the Caesar salad became ill.* **Consequently** means "therefore, as a result": *The temperature was above 90 degrees for a week; consequently, all the tomatoes burst on the vine.*

suppose to/supposed to; use to/used to Both **suppose to** and **use to** are incorrect. The preferred usage is **supposed to** or **used to:** *I was supposed to (not "suppose to") get up early this morning to go hiking in the mountains. I used to (not "use to") enjoy the seashore, but now I prefer the mountains.*

sure/surely When used as an adverb meaning **surely, sure** is considered inappropriate for formal discourse. A qualifier like "certainly" should be used instead of **sure:** *My neighbors were certainly right about it.* It is widely used, however, in speech and informal writing: *They were sure right about that car.*

sure and/sure to; try and/try to Sure to and try to are the preferred forms for formal discourse: *Be sure to (not "sure and") come home early tonight. Try to (not "try and") avoid the traffic on the interstate.*

taught/taut Taught is the past tense of "to teach": *My English teachers taught especially well.* Taut is "tightly drawn": *Pull the knot taut or it will not hold.*

than/then Than, a conjunction, is used in comparisons: *Robert is taller than Michael.* Then, an adverb, is used to indicate time: *We knew then that there was little to be gained by further discussion.*

that The conjunction that is occasionally omitted, especially after verbs of thinking, saying, believing, and so forth: *She said (that) they would come by train.* The omission of the conjunction almost always occurs when the dependent clause begins with a personal pronoun or a proper name. The omission is most frequent in informal speech and writing.

that/which Traditionally, that is used to introduce a restrictive clause: *They should buy the cookies that the neighbor's child is selling.* Which, in contrast, is used to introduce nonrestrictive clauses: *The cookies, which are covered in chocolate, would make a nice evening* *snack*. This distinction is maintained far more often in formal writing than in everyday speech, where voice can often distinguish restrictive from nonrestrictive clauses.

that/which/who **That** is used to refer to animals, things, and people: *That's my dog. I like that pen. Is that your mother?* In accepted usage, **who** is used to refer only to people: *Who is the man over there?* **Which** is used to refer only to inanimate objects and animals: *Which pen do you prefer? Which dog is the one that you would like to buy?*

their/there/they're Although these three words sound alike, they have very different meanings. **Their,** the possessive form of "they," means "belonging to them": *Their house is new.* **There** can point out place (*There is the picture I was telling you about*) or function as an expletive (*There is a mouse behind you!*) **They're** is a contraction for "they are": *They're not at home right now.*

them/those OR **these** **Them** is nonstandard when used as an adjective: *I enjoyed those (not "them") apples a great deal.*

this here/these here/that there/them there Each of these phrases is nonstandard: **this here** for "this"; **these here** for "these";

that there for "that"; **them there** for "those."

threw/thru/through **Threw,** the past tense of the verb "throw," means "to hurl an object": *He threw the ball at the batter.* **Through** means "from one end to the other" or "by way of": *They walked through the museum all afternoon.* **Through** should be used in formal writing in place of **thru,** a colloquial spelling.

thusly/thus Thusly is a pointless synonym for **thus.** Speakers and writers often use **thusly** only for a deliberately humorous effect.

till/until/'til **Till** and **until** are used interchangeably in speech and writing; **'til,** a shortened form of **until,** is rarely used.

time period The expression **time period** is redundant, since "**period**" is a period of time. *The local ambulance squad reported three emergency calls in a one-week period (not "time period").*

to/too/two Although the words sound alike, they are different parts of speech and have different meanings. **To** is a preposition indicating direction or part of an infinitive; **too** is an adverb meaning "also" or "in extreme"; and **two** is a number: *I have to go to the store to buy two items. Do you want to come too?*

too Be careful when using **too** as an intensifier in speech and writing: *The dog is too mean.* Adding an explanation of the excessive quality makes the sentence more logical: *The dog is too mean to trust alone with children.*

toward/towards The two words are used interchangeably in both formal and informal speech and writing.

track/tract Track, as a noun, is a path or course: *The railroad track in the Omaha station has recently been electrified.* **Track** as a verb, is "to follow": *Sophisticated guidance control systems are used to track the space shuttles.* **Tract** is "an expanse of land" or "a brief treatise": *Jonathan Swift wrote many tracts on the political problems of his day.*

try and/try to While **try to** is the preferred form informal speech and writing, both phrases occur in all types of speech and writing.

type/type of In written English, **type of** is the preferred construction: *This is an unusual type of flower.* In informal speech and writing, it is acceptable to use **type** immediately before a noun: *I like this type car.*

unexceptional/unexceptionable Although both **unexceptional** and **unexceptionable** are adjectives, they have different meanings and are not interchangeable. **Unexceptional**

means "commonplace, ordinary": *Despite the glowing reviews the new restaurant had received, we found it offered unexceptional meals and services.* **Unexceptionable** means "not offering any basis for exception or objection; beyond criticism": *Because of his unexceptional behavior, he did not stand out from the crowd.*

unique Since **unique** is an absolute adjective meaning "one of a kind," it cannot sensibly be used with a modifier such as "very," "most," or "extremely": *That is a unique (not "very unique" or "most unique") outfit.*

usage/use Usage is a noun that refers to the generally accepted way of doing something. The word refers especially to the conventions of language: *"Most unique" is considered incorrect usage.* Use can be either a noun or a verb. As a noun, **use** means "the act of employing or putting into service": *In the adult education course, I learned the correct use of tools.* Usage is often misused in place of the noun **use:** *Effective use (not "usage") of your time results in greater personal satisfaction.*

use/utilize/utilization Utilize means "to make use of": *They should utilize the new profit-sharing plan to decrease taxable income.* **Utilization** is the noun form of **utilize.** In most instances, however, **use** is preferred to either **utilize** or **utilization** as less overly formal and stilted: *They should use the new profit-sharing plan to decrease taxable income.*

use to could/use to be able to   The phrase **used to could** is nonstandard for **used to be able to:** *I used to be able to (not "used to could") touch my toes.*

very   The adverb **very** is sometimes used unnecessarily, especially in modifying an absolute adjective: *It was a very unique experience.* In such instances, it clearly should be omitted. Further, **very** has become overworked and lost much of its power. They suggest using more precise modifiers such as "extremely" and "especially."

want in/want out   Both phrases are informal: **want in** for "want to enter"; **want out** for "want to leave": *The dog wants to enter (not "wants in"). The cat wants to leave (not "wants out").*

way/ways   Way is the preferred usage for formal speech and writing; **ways** is used colloquially: *They have a little way (not "ways") to go before they reach the campground.*

when/where   Where and when are not interchangeable: *Weekends are occasions when* *(not "where") we have a chance to spend time with the family.*

where at/where to Both phrases are generally considered to be too informal to be acceptable in good writing and speech: *Where is John? (not "Where is John at?") Where is Mike going? (not "Where is Mike going to?")*

where/that Where and that are not interchangeable: *We see by the memo that (not "where") overtime has been discontinued.*

which/witch Which is a pronoun meaning "what one": *Which desk is yours?* Witch is a noun meaning "a person who practices magic": *The superstitious villagers accused her of being a witch.*

who/whoever; whom/whomever Traditionally, **who/whoever** is used as a subject (the nominative case) and **whom/whomever** as an object (the objective case). In informal speech and writing, however, since **who** and **whom** often occur at the beginning of a sentence, people usually select **who,** regardless of grammatical function.

without/unless Without is a dialectical or regional use of **unless.**

with regards to/with regard to/as regards Use **with regard to** or **as regards** in place of **with regards to** in formal speech and writing: *As regards your inquiry, we have asked our shipping department to hold the merchandise until Monday.*

womanly/womanlike/womanish All three words mean having traits or qualities characteristic of or appropriate to adult human females. Nonetheless, each carries a different shade of meaning. **Womanly** is a term of approval. As such, it connotes admirable traits such as self-possession, modesty, and nurturing: *She evinced a womanly consideration for others.* **Womanlike** can be a neutral synonym for **womanly,** or it can convey mild disapproval: *Her womanlike tears revealed her lack of spirit.* **Womanish** is usually disparaging. When applied to women, it suggests that they possess socially unacceptable traits: *Her character was marred by a womanish stubbornness.* When applied to men, it suggests that they show traits unacceptable in men but (in what is regarded as a sexist notion) typical of women: *He has a womanish softness to his hands.*

who's/whose **Who's** is the contraction for "who is": *Who's the person in charge here?* **Whose** is the possessive form of **who:** *"Whose book is this?*

would have Do not use the phrase **would have** in place of **had** in clauses that begin with "if" and express a state contrary to fact: *If the driver had (not "would have") been wearing his seat belt, he would have escaped without injury.*

would of/could of There is no such expression as **would of** or **could of**: *He would have (not "would of") gone.* Also, **of** is not a substitute for " 've,": *She would've (not "would of") left earlier.*

you was You was is nonstandard for **you were**: *You were (not "you was") late on Thursday.*

your/you're Your is the possessive form of "you": *Your book is overdue at the library.* **You're** is the contraction of "you are": *You're just the person we need for this job.*

Section III

Punctuation

Punctuation is intended to clarify the meaning of writing. It provides the key to the logic of an argument; for example, when readers see a semicolon in a work, they know the writer is linking closely related ideas. The ability to use different forms of punctuation to express ideas gives variety, coherence, and strength to writing.

End punctuation: period, question mark, exclamation point

Period

Use a period to end sentences that are statements, indirect questions, or mild commands. Also use a period after most abbreviations and within decimal numbers and amounts of money.

Use a period with:

Statements

EXAMPLES:

The mayor's speech was unusually well received.

The meeting was amicable and important.

Indirect questions

An indirect question reports what a person has asked, but not in the speaker's original words. Since the question is paraphrased, quotation marks are not used.

EXAMPLES:

He asked me when the train will leave the station.

She wanted to know whether the supplies would be back in stock by Tuesday.

Mild commands

If you cannot decide whether to use a period or an exclamation mark after a command, use a period. Exclamation marks are used infrequently in formal writing.

EXAMPLES:

Read the next two chapters before Tuesday.

Please leave your muddy shoes on the mat outside the door.

Most abbreviations

EXAMPLES:

H. Sammis & Sons, Inc. recently issued its annual report.

A. L. Smith just returned from a convention at the U.S. Department of Agriculture.

When a sentence ends with an abbreviation, use only one period.

EXAMPLES:

The meeting will begin promptly at 8 A.M.

I will send your files to Jeffrey Mallack, M.D.

Also note that the official two-letter postal zip code state abbreviations do not use periods. Acronyms—abbreviations formed from the first letters of the words in a name—never use periods.

EXAMPLES:

Acronyms:

UNICEF   UNESCO   USMC   /
DDT   IBM   FCC   IRS   NASA
NATO

Zip code state abbreviations:

NY   PA   CA   ME   MD

Within decimal numbers and amounts of money

EXAMPLES:

A sales tax of 7.5 percent is leveled on all clothing in this state.

He spent $44.50 on the shirt, $36.99 on the pants, and $22.00 on the tie.

Question mark

Use a question mark to end a sentence, clause, phrase, or single word that asks a direct question. Also use a question mark within parentheses to indicate uncertainty about the correctness of a number or date included within the sentence.

Use a question mark:

To indicate a question

EXAMPLES:

Who invited him to the party?

"Is something the matter?" she asked.

Whom shall we elect? Murry? Harris?

To indicate doubt about information

EXAMPLES:

Socrates was born in 470 (?) B.C.

The codex dates back to 500 (?) A.D.

Exclamation point

Use an exclamation point to end a sentence, clause, phrase, or single word that expresses strong emotion, such as surprise, command, admiration, and so forth.

Use an exclamation mark to express:

Strong emotion

EXAMPLES:

Go away!

What a week this has been!

Punctuation within a sentence: comma, semicolon, colon, dash, ellipsis, parentheses, brackets, quotation marks, italics/underlining, solidus (slash)

Comma

The comma is the most often used mark of punctuation within a sentence. In general, commas separate parts of a sentence. Adding unnecessary commas or omitting necessary ones can confuse a reader and obscure the meaning of a sentence.

Use a comma:

To separate independent clauses of a compound sentence linked by a coordinating conjunction and, but, yet, for, or, or nor, unless the compound sentence is very brief

EXAMPLES:

Longer sentences:

Almost any person knows how to earn money, yet not one in a million knows how to spend it.

Bill is not in the office today, but he will be here tomorrow.

Shorter sentences:

We must catch the train or we will miss the meeting.

Mark washed the dishes and Jim dried.

To set off most introductory elements

An introductory element modifies (describes) a word or words in the independent clause that follows.

EXAMPLES:

Having rid themselves of their former

rulers, the people now disagreed on the new leadership.

Although the details have not been fully developed, scientists are confident that people will reach the stars.

Politically, our candidate has proved to be inept.

Hurt, she left the room quickly.

Pleased with the result, he appraised his work.

The comma can be omitted after brief introductory prepositional and infinitive phrases and subordinate clauses if it is not needed for clarity.

EXAMPLES:

Comma unnecessary:

As a child he was intractable.

Comma is necessary for clarification:

In 1988, 300 people won in the lottery.

To set off nonrestrictive elements

Since it restricts, or limits the meaning of, the word or words it applies to, a **restrictive** element is essential to the meaning of the sentence and thus cannot be omitted.

The novel that she wrote in 1989 won a literary award.

Employees who started before November 1 will be entitled to two more vacation days per year.

Since it adds information about the word or words it applies to but does not limit that meaning, a **nonrestrictive** element can be left out of a sentence without changing the meaning. Place commas before and after the nonrestrictive portion.

EXAMPLES:

Her most recent novel, written in 1989, won a literary award.

Our new car, which has whitewall tires and a leather interior, will be ready for delivery on Thursday.

To set off interrupting words or phrases.

There are several different kinds of interrupters. These include words of direct address, appositives, contrasting expressions, interjections, parenthetical expressions, and transitional words.

Words of direct address: These are words that tell to whom a comment is addressed.

You realize, Mary, that we may never
return to Paris.

Jim, where have you been?

Appositives: Appositives are words that give
additional information about the preceding or
following word or expression. Many appositives are nonrestrictive and are thus set off
from the rest of the sentence, usually with
commas. Be careful not to set off restrictive
appositives, which are necessary for the
meaning of the sentence.

EXAMPLES:

Nonrestrictive appositives:

A heavy sleeper, my sister is the last to
awaken.

The last to awake is my sister, a heavy
sleeper.

My sister, a heavy sleeper, is the last to
awaken.

March, the month of crocuses, can still bring
snow and ice.

His favorite author, Stephen King, entered
the auditorium.

Mr. Case, a member of the committee, refused to comment.

Restrictive appositives:

My friend Mary spoke at the convention.

The crowd fell silent as the author Stephen King entered the auditorium.

Contrasting expressions: Use commas to set off groups of words that show contrast.

EXAMPLES:

The boys, not the men, did most of the chores around the house.

His clever wit, not his appearance, won him many friends.

This report needs more facts, less fluff.

Interjections: Use a comma to set off any interjection. Examples of interjections include *well, my, oh, yes, no,* and so forth.

EXAMPLES:

Oh, here's our new neighbor.

Why, you can't mean that!

Well, can you imagine that!

Parenthetical expressions: Use commas to set off expressions that explain by providing additional information.

EXAMPLES:

You may, if you insist, demand a retraction.

If you wouldn't mind, please leave your raincoat and umbrella on the porch.

Transitional words: Transitional expressions include *however, indeed, consequently, as a result, of course, for example, in fact,* and so forth. Use a comma to distinguish these expressions from the rest of the sentence.

EXAMPLES:

Still, you must agree that he knows his business.

The use of pesticides, however, has its disadvantages.

He knew, nevertheless, that all was lost.

To separate items in a series

Use a comma to separate words, phrases, and clauses that are part of a series of three or more items.

EXAMPLES:

The Danes are an industrious, friendly, generous, and hospitable people.

The chief agricultural products of Denmark are butter, eggs, potatoes, beets, wheat, barley, and oats.

It is permissible to omit the final comma before the "and" in a series of words as long as the absence of a comma does not interfere with clarity of meaning. In many cases, however, the inclusion or omission of the comma can significantly affect the meaning of the sentence. In the following sentence, omission of the final comma might indicate that the tanks were amphibious: Their equipment included airplanes, helicopters, artillery, amphibious vehicles, and tanks.

As a general rule, the final comma is never wrong, and it always helps the reader see that the last two items are separate.

Do not use commas to separate two items treated as a single unit within a series, as in this example:

For breakfast he ordered orange juice, bread and butter, coffee, and bacon and eggs.

But when the items are treated individually, each is separated by a comma, as in this sentence:

At the supermarket he bought orange juice, bread, butter, bacon, and eggs.

Do not use commas to separate adjectives

that are so closely related that they appear to form a single element with the noun they modify. Adjectives that refer to the number, age *(old, young, new)*, size, color, or location of the noun often fall within this category. To determine whether or not to use the comma in these instances, insert the word *and*. If *and* cannot replace the comma without creating an awkward sentence, it is safe to conclude that a comma is also out of place.

EXAMPLES:

twenty happy little youngsters

a dozen large blue dresses

several dingy old Western mining towns

beautiful tall white birches

But commas must be used when each adjective is considered separately, not as modifiers of other adjectives:

EXAMPLES:

the beautiful, expensive dress

the happy, smiling youngsters

He sold his business, rented his house, gave up his car, paid his creditors, and set off for Alaska.

They strolled along the city streets,

browsed in the bookshops, and dined at their favorite café.

To separate parts of dates, addresses, geographical locations, titles of individuals, and long numbers

EXAMPLES:

The Declaration of Independence was signed on July 4, 1776.

Pearl Harbor was bombed on Sunday, December 7, 1941.

Her friend lives at 35 Fifth Avenue, New York, N.Y.

She moved from 1515 Halsted Street, Chicago, Illinois.

He lived in Lima, Peru, for fifteen years.

Dr. Martin Price, Dean of Admissions, is in the office down the hall.

This is Mr. John Winthrop, President.

The population of Grove City, Minnesota, is 34,500.

If you win this week's jackpot, the payoff is $75,000.00!

To set off quoted matter from the rest of the sentence

(see also ''Quotation Marks,'' page 291.)

EXAMPLE:

He said, ''I wish you had been at the workshop today.''

She replied, ''Unfortunately, my meeting ran late.''

''Unfortunately,'' she replied, ''my meeting ran late.''

To set off the salutation of a personal letter and the complimentary close of a personal or a formal letter

EXAMPLES:

Dear Midge,

Very truly yours,

To denote an omitted word or words in one or more parallel constructions within a sentence

EXAMPLE:

John is studying Greek; George, Latin.

To prevent misreading

The comma tells the reader to stop briefly before reading on. Words may run together in confusing ways unless you use a comma to separate them. Use a comma in such sentences even though no rule requires one.

A comma is used in the following sentence even though a short introductory phrase does not normally require one: Soon after, she quit the job for good.

The next sentence requires a comma because it seems incomplete without one: The people who can, usually contribute some money to the local holiday drive.

Semicolon

In general, a semicolon is used to separate parts of a sentence, such as independent clauses, items in a series, and explanations or summaries from the main clause. In choosing among the three punctuation marks that separate main clauses—the comma, the semicolon, and the colon—a writer needs to decide on the relationship between ideas. A semicolon can be used to great effect when the first clause sets up some expectation in the reader that a related idea is to follow. The semicolon then gives a brief stop before the second clause completes the thought.

In general:

The comma	links both equal and un-equal sentence parts.
The semicolon	links equal and balanced sentence parts.
The colon	links unequal sentence parts.

Use a semicolon:

To separate independent clauses not joined by a simple conjunction

(See p. 265 for the use of a comma with independent clauses joined by simple conjunctions.)

EXAMPLE:

The house burned down; it was the last shattering blow.

The war must continue; we will be satisfied only with victory.

We have made several attempts to reach you by telephone; not a single call has been returned.

To separate independent clauses joined by a conjunctive adverb such as however, nevertheless, otherwise, therefore, besides, hence, indeed, instead, nonetheless, still, then or *thus*

EXAMPLE:

The funds are inadequate; therefore, the
project will close down.

Enrollments exceed all expectations;
however, there is a teacher shortage.

He knew the tickets for the performance
would be scarce; therefore, he arrived at
the concert hall two hours early.

A comma is generally used after a conjunctive after a conjunctive adverb. Commas are
optional, however, with such one-syllable conjunctive adverbs as *thus* and *hence;* they are
frequently omitted as well when *therefore, instead,* or any of several other conjunctive adverbs are placed at the end of clauses.

EXAMPLE:

She skipped her lunch; thus she was
ravenously hungry by 4:00.

He did not take notes; he borrowed hers
instead.

*To separate long or possibly ambiguous
items in a series, especially when those items
already include commas*

EXAMPLE:

The elected officers are Robert Harris,
president; Charles Lawrence, vice

president; Samantha Jill, treasurer; and Elisabeth Fink, secretary.

During the parade, the marchers wore red, green, and blue uniforms; carried silver banners; and sang songs.

To precede an abbreviation or word that introduces an explanation or summary

EXAMPLE:

On the advice of his broker, he chose to invest in major industries; i.e., steel, automobiles, and oil.

She organizes her work well; for example, by putting correspondence in folders of different colors to indicate degrees of urgency.

Colon

As a mark of introduction, the colon tells the reader that the first statement is going to be explained by the second or signals that a quotation or series will follow. In effect, the colon is a substitute for such phrases as *for example* and *namely*. A colon can often be interchanged with a dash, although a dash indicates a less formal and more abrupt shift.

Use a colon:

To introduce a long formal statement, summary, explanation, quotation, or question

EXAMPLES:

Formal statement:
This I believe: All men are created equal and must enjoy equally the rights that are inalienably theirs.

Summary:
They cannot pay their monthly bills because their money is tied up in their stocks and bonds: they are paper-rich and cash-poor.

Explanation:
It is a good thing to be old early: to have the fragility and sensitivity of the old, and a bit of wisdom, before the years of planning and building have run out.—Martin Gumbert

Quotation:
Richards replied: "You are right. There can be no unilateral peace just as there can be no unilateral war. No one contests that view." (Note: Use a comma, not a colon, if the quotation is a single sentence.)

Question:
This is the issue: Can an employer dismiss an employee simply because the employee laughs loudly? (Note that the first word of

the sentence following the colon is capitalized. This applies to formal statements as well as to questions.)

To introduce a series or list of items, examples, or the like

EXAMPLES:

The three committees are as follows: membership, finance, and nominations.

He named his five favorite poets: Byron, Keats, Tennyson, Hardy, and Dickinson.

It is impossible to dissociate language from science or science from language, because every natural science always involves three things: the sequence of phenomena on which the science is based, the abstract concepts which call these phenomena to mind; and the words in which the concepts are expressed.—Antoine Lavoisier

The colon should not be used after *of* or after a verb.

EXAMPLES:

The committee consisted of nine teachers, twelve parents, and six business leaders.

Possible choices include games, tapes, books, and puzzles.

To follow the salutation of a formal letter or speech

EXAMPLES:

Dear Mr. Brodwin:

My fellow Americans:

To Whom It May Concern:

To follow the name of the speaker in a play

EXAMPLES:

Ghost: Revenge his foul and most unnatural murder.

Hamlet: Murder?

To separate parts of a citation

EXAMPLES:

Genesis 3:2

Journal of Transcendentalism 15:251–255

To separate hours from minutes in indicating time

EXAMPLES:

1:30 P.M.

12:30 A.M.

Dash

A dash is used to show sudden changes in thought or to set off certain sentence elements. Like the exclamation point, dashes are dramatic and thus should be used sparingly in formal writing. Do not confuse the dash with the hyphen (see page 304 on the hyphen).

Use a dash to:

Mark an abrupt change in thought, shift in tone, or grammatical construction in the middle of a sentence

EXAMPLES:

He won the game—but I'm getting ahead of the story.

She told me—does she really mean it?—that she will inform us of any changes ahead of time from now on.

Suggest halting or hesitant speech

EXAMPLES:

''Well—er—it's hard to explain,'' he faltered.

Madame de Vionnett instantly rallied.

"And you know—though it might occur to one—it isn't in the least that he's ashamed of her. She's really—in a way—extremely good looking."—Henry James

Indicate a sudden break or interruption before a sentence is completed

EXAMPLES:

"Harvey, don't climb up that—." It was too late.

If they discovered the truth—he did not want to think of the consequences.

Add emphasis to parenthetical material or mark an emphatic separation between parenthetical material and the rest of the sentence

EXAMPLES:

His influence—he was a powerful figure in the community—was a deterrent to effective opposition.

The car he was driving—a gleaming red convertible—was the most impressive thing about him.

To set off an appositive or an appositive phrase when a comma would provide less than the desired emphasis on the appositive or when the use of commas might result in confusion because of commas within the appositive phrase

EXAMPLES:

The premier's promise of changes—land reform and higher wages—was not easily fulfilled.

The qualities Renoir valued in his painting—rich shadows, muted colors, graceful figures—flourished in the ballet dancers he used as subjects.

To replace an offensive word or part of one.

EXAMPLE:

Where the h— is he?

Where's that son of a —?

Ellipsis

The ellipsis mark consists of three spaced periods (. . .). Use it to show that part of a quotation has been left out. You can also use the ellipsis in place of a dash to indicate pauses and unfinished statements in quoted speech.

Use an ellipsis to:

Show that part of a quote has been omitted, to indicate pauses and unfinished statements

Original paragraph:

He left his home in the city at age twenty. Seeking solitude, he built a log cabin in the mountains. Years later he returned to the city to find that everything had changed.

Quoted portions:

He left his home in the city at age twenty. . . . Years later he returned to find that everything had changed. (Ellipsis indicates the omission of the second sentence. Notice that the period is retained, resulting in four spaced periods.)

He left his home. . . . Seeking solitude, he built a cabin in the mountains. (Ellipsis indicates omission at the end of the first sentence. The period from the end of the sentence follows the ellipsis marks.)

Parentheses

Parentheses are used to enclose nonessential material within a sentence. This can include facts, explanations, digressions, and examples that may be helpful but are not necessary for the sentence. Do not put a comma before a parentheses.

Use parentheses to

Enclose material that is not part of the main sentence but is too important to omit

EXAMPLES:

Faulkner's novels (published by Random House) were selected as prizes in the recent contest.

The data (see Table 14) were very impressive.

To enclose part of a sentence that would be confusing if enclosed by commas

EXAMPLE:

The authors he advised (none other than Hemingway, Lewis, and Cather) would have been delighted to honor him today.

To enclose an explanatory item that is not part of the statement or sentence

EXAMPLE:

He wrote to *The Paris* (Illinois) *News*.

To enclose numbers or letters that designate each item in a series

EXAMPLE:

The project is (1) too time-consuming, (2) too expensive, and (3) poorly staffed.

To enclose a numerical figure used to confirm a spelled-out number that comes before it

EXAMPLE:

Enclosed is a check for ten dollars ($10.00) to cover the cost of the order.

Dashes, commas, and parentheses can all be used to set off information that is not essential to the sentence. Consult the following chart for a quick review of the different effects each mark will achieve in your writing. Then select the specific mark that creates the emphasis your ideas require.

Dashes create the most emphasis

Many workers—including those in the mail room—distrust the new shipping regulations.

Commas create less emphasis

Many workers, including those in the mail room, distrust the new shipping regulations.

Parentheses create the least emphasis

Many workers (including those in the mail room) distrust the new shipping regulations.

Brackets

Brackets are used in pairs to enclose figures, phrases, or sentences, most often within a direct quotation.

Use brackets to:

Explain, clarify, or correct the contents of a direct quotation

EXAMPLES:

According to the Globe critic, "This [*Man and Superman*] is one of Shaw's greatest plays."

"Young as they are," he writes, "these students are afflicted with cynicism, world-weariness, and *a total disregard for tradition and authority.*" [Emphasis is mine.]

"As a result of the Gemini V mission [the flight by astronauts Cooper and Conrad in August 1965], we have proof that human beings can withstand the eight days in space required for a round trip to the moon.''

"It was on August 25, 1944 [1945—Ed.] that delegates representing forty-six countries met in San Francisco.''

Indicate that an error in fact, spelling, punctuation, or language usage is quoted deliberately in an effort to reproduce the original statement with complete accuracy

To indicate the questionable expression, place the Latin word *"sic,"* meaning "thus," directly after it in brackets.

EXAMPLES:

"George Washington lived during the seventeenth [sic] century.''

"The governor of Missisipi [sic] addressed the student body.''

Enclose stage directions for a play

EXAMPLE:

Juliet: [*Snatching Romeo's dagger*] . . . Oh happy dagger! This is thy sheath; [*Stabs herself*] there rest and let me die.

Enclose comments made in a verbatim transcript

EXAMPLE:

Sen. Eaton: The steady rise in taxes must be halted. [Applause]

Substitute for parentheses with material already enclosed by parentheses

Although this use is not encountered frequently, it is sometimes used in footnotes.

EXAMPLE:

¹See "Rene Descartes" (M. C. Beardsley, *The European Philosophers from Descartes to Nietzsche* [New York, 1960]).

To enclose the publication date, inserted by the editor, of an item appearing in an earlier issue of a periodical

This is used in letters to the editor or in articles written on subjects previously reported. Parentheses may be used instead.

EXAMPLES:

Dear Sir: Your excellent article on China [April 15] brings to mind my recent experience . . .

When removing old wallpaper

[*Homeowners' Monthly*, June 1990], some
do-it-yourselfers neglect to . . .

Quotation Marks

The main function of quotation marks is to enclose a direct quotation. Quotation marks are
always used in pairs to mark the beginning and
end of the quotation.

Punctuating with quotation marks is largely
a matter of common sense: if a colon, semicolon, question mark, or exclamation point is
part of the quotation, place it *inside* the end
quotation mark, if it is not part of the quotation, place it *outside*.

Before a colon or semicolon: Place the end
quotation mark *before* a colon or semicolon, as
in the following example: He remembered that
the boys had always called Tom "the champ";
he began to wonder if the reputation had endured.

After a question mark or exclamation point:
Place the end quotation mark *after* a question
mark or exclamation point only when the question or exclamation is part of the quoted passage, as in this example: "Hurry, please,
before it is too late!" she cried. In all other
cases, place the end quotation mark *before* the
question mark or exclamation point, as shown
in this example: Did Pangloss really mean it

when he said, "This is the best of all possible worlds"?

Use quotation marks to:

Indicate a direction quotation

Use double quotation marks to enclose a direct quotation.

EXAMPLE:

"They've come back!" she exclaimed.

"It's not in the cabinet; it's on the counter," my sister shouted out.

Use single quotation marks to enclose a quotation within a quotation.

EXAMPLE:

Reading Jill's letter, Pat said "Listen to this! 'I've just received notice that I made the dean's list.' Isn't that great?"

As in the above examples, use a comma between the quotation and phrases such as *according to the speaker, he said, she replied,* used to introduce or conclude a quotation.

If a quotation consists of two or more consecutive paragraphs, use quotation marks at the beginning of each paragraph, but place them at the end of the last paragraph only.

Mark words or groups of words that are quoted from the original

EXAMPLES:

Portia's speech on ''the quality of mercy'' is one of the most quoted passages from Shakespeare.

It was Shaw who wrote: ''All great truths begin as blasphemies.''

Enclose titles of newspaper and magazine articles, essays, short stories, poems, chapters of books, songs, works of art, and radio and television programs

The quotation marks are designed to distinguish the literary pieces from the books or periodicals (these are underlined or italicized) in which they appear.

EXAMPLES:

Our anthology contains such widely assorted pieces as Bacon's essay ''Of Studies,'' Poe's ''The Gold Bug,'' Keats's ''Ode to the West Wind,'' and an article on criticism from *The New Yorker*.

Most people recognize Da Vinci's ''Mona Lisa'' and Rodin's ''The Thinker.''

He especially enjoyed watching reruns of

"All in the Family" and "My Mother, the Car."

Use quotation marks around the titles of plays only if they are part of a larger collection. Referred to as single volumes, they are underlined or italicized.

EXAMPLE

"The Wild Duck" is the Ibsen play included in this edition of *Modern European Plays*.

Enclose the names of ships and airplanes. Italics and underlines can also be used

EXAMPLES:

Lindbergh called the airplane in which he flew across the Atlantic the "Spirit of St. Louis."

We had waited our entire lives for a chance to take a cruise on the "Queen Elizabeth."

Emphasize a word or phrase that is the subject of discussion or to suggest a word or phrase is being used ironically

EXAMPLES:

The words "imply" and "infer" are not synonymous.

Such Freudian terms as "ego," "superego," "id," and "libido" have now entered popular usage and are familiar to most Americans.

The radio blasting forth Kim's favorite "music" is to his parents an instrument of torture.

Bob's skiing "vacation" consisted of three weeks with his leg in a cast.

Italics/Underlining

Italics are used to emphasize or set apart specific words and phrases. In handwritten or typed papers, underlining indicates italics.

Use italics (underlining) to:

Distinguish titles of books, newspapers, long poems, magazines, pamphlets, published speeches, long musical compositions, movies, plays, works of art, ships, and aircraft

EXAMPLES:

I read *War and Peace, Beowulf,* and Lincoln's *Gettysburg Address* as part of my annual summer self-improvement kick.

They enjoyed the original version of

Invasion of the Boby Snatchers far more than the remake.

Set off foreign words and phrases that are not in common use

EXAMPLES:

In his younger days he was quite a *bon vivant*.

I'll be there, *deo volente*.

Refer to a word, letter, number, or expression used as such

Quotation marks are sometimes used instead.

EXAMPLES:

She drew a large *3* on the blackboard.

The word *fantastic* is his favorite adjective.

Do not pronounce the final *e* in *Hecate*.

Indicate stage directions within brackets

EXAMPLE:

Heidi [*turning to Anita*]: Did he call me?

Anita: I didn't hear him. [*She picks up a magazine*.]

Emphasize specific words and phrases

Occasionally, italics can be used to stress certain words and phrases.

EXAMPLE:

The man was *totally* bereft; he had neither friends nor relatives to lend a hand.

Solidus (Slash)

The solidus acts as a dividing line, as in dates and fractions, and in run-in passages of poetry to show verse division; it is also used between two words to indicate an option.

Use a solidus to:

Separate lines of poetry within the text

When used in this way, the solidus marks the end of a line of poetry and has equal space on either side

EXAMPLE:

William Blake's stanza on anger in "A Poison Tree" seems as appropriate today as when it was first written: "I was angry with my friend: / I told my wrath, my wrath did end. / I was angry with my foe: / I told it not, my wrath did grow."

Indicate dates and fractions

EXAMPLES:

winter 1990/1991

the fiscal year 1992/93

3/4 + 2/3

$x/y - y/x$

Indicate options and alternatives

EXAMPLE:

I have never seen the advantage of pass/fail courses.

Note: Try to avoid using he/she. Instead, make the subject plural (''they'') or revise the construction completely.

Punctuation within a word: apostrophe, hyphen

Apostrophe

In contrast to other marks of punctuation, which divide words from one another, the apostrophe (') is used within a word to show the omission of one or more letters, to show possession, or (in some cases) to indicate a plural.

Use an apostrophe to:

Denote the omission of one or more letters, figures, or numerals

Apostrophes are used to form contractions

EXAMPLES:

I am	I'm
you are	you're

he is	he's
she is	she's
they are	they're
we are	we're
it is	it's
who is	who's
cannot	can't
could not	couldn't
was not	wasn't
were not	weren't
would not	wouldn't
is not	isn't
madam	ma'am
of the clock	o'clock

Note: Will not is irregular; the contraction is "won't"

EXAMPLES:

The Spirit of **'76**

The class of **'70**

Indicate the omission of letters in quoted dialogue

EXAMPLES:

'tis a fine day

goin' fishing

Show the possessive case of nouns, indicating ownership

To form the possessive of most singular and

plural nouns and indefinite pronouns not ending in *s*, add an apostrophe and *s*.

EXAMPLES:

"The **Monk's Tale**" is one of **Chaucer's Canterbury Tales.**

When he would arrive at **Mary's** house was anybody's quess.

He was amazed to find that the **women's** shoes cost fifty dollars, but the **children's** shoes cost even more.

To form the possessive of *singular* nouns (both common and proper) ending in *s* or the sound of *s*, add an apostrophe and *s* unless the addition of the *s* would sound or look awkward.

EXAMPLES:

With the ''S'' *added:*

the **horse's** mane

the **bus's** light

the **class's** average

Kansas's schools

Texas's governor

Francis's promotion

Without the ''S'' *added:*

Socrates' concepts

for old **times'** sake

for **goodness'** sake

Dickens' book

To form the possessive of *plural* nouns (both common and proper) ending in *s* or the sound of *s*, add only an apostrophe.

EXAMPLES:

farmers' problems

students' views

critics' reviews

two **weeks'** vacation

judges' opinions

the **Smiths'** travels

the **Joneses'** relatives

three **months'** delay

To form the possessive of *plural* nouns (both common and proper) not ending in *s*, add an apostrophe and *s*.

EXAMPLES:

men's clothing

children's toys

women's hats

people's observations

To form the possessive of compound words or two or more proper names, add an apostrophe and s to the last word of the compound.

EXAMPLES:

anyone **else's** property

brother-in-law's job

one **another's** books

editor-in-chief's pen

Japan and Germany's agreement

Lewis and Clark's expedition

the **University of South Carolina's** mascot

Note: Never use an apostrophe with a possessive personal pronoun. These personal pronouns are already possessive and therefore have no need for an apostrophe: *my, mine, your, yours, her, hers, its, our, ours, their,* and *theirs.*

Form the plurals of numbers, symbols, letters and words used to name themselves (add an apostrophe and an s)

EXAMPLES:

Dot the **i's** and cross the **t's**

33 **r.p.m.'s**

figure **8's**

+ 's and **−** 's

GI's

V.I.P.'s

PX's

the **1890's** (or **1890s**)
t's

Hyphen

Although a hyphen and a dash may appear to be the same at first glance, they are two very different marks of punctuation. Their form is as different as their meaning, a dash being twice as long as a hyphen. Dashes are used to separate or connect *sentence* elements; hyphens are used to separate or connect *word* elements.

Use a hyphen:

To spell out a word or name

EXAMPLES:

r-e-a-s-o-n

G-a-e-l-i-c

To divide a word into syllables

EXAMPLES:
EXAMPLES:

spec-ta-to-ri-al

liv-id-ness

*To mark the division of a word of more
than one syllable at the end of a line,
indicating that the word is to be completed
on the next line*

Do not leave a single letter at the end of a
line or fewer than three letters at the beginning of a line. Do not divide one-syllable words.

EXAMPLE:

It is difficult to estimate the damaging
psychological effects of poverty.

Avoid confusing word divisions. Certain words,
when divided, will form pronounceable units
that might confuse the reader. In these instances, do not divide the word.

*To separate the parts (when spelling out nu-
merals) of a compound number from twenty-
one to ninety-nine*

EXAMPLES:

thirty-six inches to the yard

Fifty-second Street

nineteen hundred **forty-three**

To express decades in words

EXAMPLES:

the **nineteen-twenties**

the **eighteen-sixties**

To separate (when spelling out numerals) the numerator from the denominator of a fraction, especially a fraction that is used as an adjective

EXAMPLES:

One-third cup of milk

a **three-fifths** majority

While some writers avoid hyphenating fractions used as nouns, the practice persists.

EXAMPLES:

Three fourths (or **three-fourths**) of his constituents

One fifth (**one-fifth**) of the class

Do not use a hyphen to indicate a fraction if either the numerator or the denominator is already hyphenated.

EXAMPLES:

one **thirty-second**

twenty-one thirty-sixths

To form certain compound nouns

EXAMPLES:

secretary-treasurer

cease-fire

city-state

do-gooder

AFL-CIO

has-been

Do not hyphenate compound nouns indicating chemical terms, military rank, or certain governmental positions.

EXAMPLES:

sodium chloride

vice admiral

attorney general

To combine the elements of a compound modifier when used before the noun it modifies

In most cases the same modifier is not hyphenated if it follows the noun it modifies.

EXAMPLES:

They engage in **hand-to-hand** combat.

They fought **hand to hand.**

They endured a **hand-to-mouth** existence.

They lived **hand to mouth.**

well-known expert

an expert who is **well known.**

Do not hyphenate a compound modifier that includes an adverb ending in *-ly* even when it is used before the noun.

EXAMPLES:

his **loose-fitting** jacket

his **loosely fitting** jacket

a **well-guarded** secret

a **carefully guarded** secret

To distinguish a less common pronunciation or meaning of a word from its more customary usage

EXAMPLES:

a **recreation** hall	**re-creation** of a scene
to **recover** from an illness	**re-cover** the sofa
to **reform** a sinner	**re-form** their lines

To prevent possible confusion in pronunciation if a prefix results in the doubling of a letter, especially a vowel

EXAMPLES:

anti-inflationary

co-ordinate

co-op

pre-empt

re-enact

re-election

To combine the following prefixes with proper nouns or adjectives

EXAMPLES:

anti-	anti-American	anti-British
mid-	mid-Victorian	mid-Atlantic
neo-	neo-Nazi	neo-Darwinism
non-	non-European	non-Asian
pan-	pan-American	Pan-Slavic

| pro- | pro-French | pro-American |
| un- | un-American | un-British |

To combine the following prefixes and suffixes with the main word of the compound

EXAMPLES:

co-	co-chair	co-person
ex-	ex-sergeant	ex-premier
self-	self-preservation	self-defeating
-elect	president-elect	governor-elect

To form most compound nouns and adjectives that begin with the word element listed below

Consult a dictionary for words not listed.

EXAMPLES:

cross-	cross-examine	cross-stitch
double-	double-breasted	double-park
great-	great-grandfather	great-grandchild
heavy-	heavy-handed	heavy-hearted
ill-	ill-organized	ill-timed
light-	light-fingered	light-year
single-	single-minded	single-handed
well-	well-behaved	well-wisher

Index

About the Author

LAURIE ROZAKIS received her Ph.D. in American and English Literature with distinction from State University of New York—Stony Brook in 1984. Aside from teaching full time on the university level, Dr. Rozakis has written a wide variety of scholarly and instructional material. Her latest work includes books and ancillary materials for McDougal, Littell and company; Prentice Hall; ARCO; Glenco/Macmillan/McGraw-Hill; IBM; and Scholastic. Her latest texts include the *Verbal Workbook for the ACT*, *The College Writing Placement and Proficiency Examination*, and *The Advanced Placement Examination in English*. She resides in New York with her husband and two children.